ONE HUNDRED SPECIES AND ONE FAMILY TREE

MY LOVE SONG

ONE HUNDRED SPECIES AND ONE FAMILY TREE

MY LOVE SONG

WILLIAM MOLDWIN

Kravitz & Sons

INNOVATORS IN PUBLISHING, MARKETING AND ADVERTISING

Kravitz and Sons LLC
204 E Arlington Blvd. Suite B
Greenville, NC 27858

Published by Kravitz and Sons LLC.

ISBN: 979-8-89639-404-4 (sc)
ISBN: 979-8-89639-403-7 (e)

Library of Congress Control Number: 2025917174

One Hundred Species and One Family Tree: My Love Song
By: William Moldwin

A Moving Tribute to Nature, Family, and the Interconnectedness of All Life

In *One Hundred Species and One Family Tree:* My Love Song by William Moldwin is a beautifully written, deeply thoughtful blend of memoir, nature writing, and spiritual reflection. What makes this book exceptional is not only its unique concept, intertwining the stories of over 100 tree species with a personal family narrative, but also the heart and authenticity with which it is told.

Moldwin, a retired pastor and amateur botanist, brings his two-acre Michigan property to life through rich, observational storytelling. He introduces readers to the trees and plants that fill his garden and woodland, sharing fascinating insights about their origins, their medicinal properties, and even their secret ways of communicating underground. Alongside this naturalist's lens, Moldwin weaves his own history: the story of a boy raised by Hungarian immigrant parents, shaped by their struggles, wisdom, and love.

This dual focus, on trees and on family, gives the book a rare emotional depth. Just as roots connect trees underground, Moldwin reminds us how families and generations are linked, even when separated by time or hardship. The "family tree" becomes both literal and metaphorical; a brilliant narrative device that ties together his love for nature and his reverence for human connection.

What's truly remarkable is the gentleness of Moldwin's voice. His prose is humble, wise, and reflective. He doesn't seek to impress, but rather to share, to invite the reader into a quiet space of appreciation for the world's living beauty and for the stories that shape our lives. Whether he's describing the bark of a sycamore or reflecting on aging and faith, the tone is meditative and grounding.

This book is a soothing experience, a kind of literary walk in the woods. It's perfect for readers who love memoirs rooted in place, who enjoy nature writing in the tradition of Annie Dillard or Robin Wall Kimmerer, or who seek spiritual encouragement from the natural world. Moldwin's reflections on faith, family, and mortality are handled with honesty and grace, making this a meaningful read for those going through seasons of transition or contemplation.

Verdict:

One Hundred Species and One Family Tree is more than a nature guide or personal memoir; it's a heartfelt love song to life, connection, and God's creation. William Moldwin's quiet wisdom and sincere voice resonate long after the final page. This is the kind of book you return to, not just to remember the facts, but to revisit the feeling it gave you: peace, reverence, and gratitude.

Rating: ★★★★★ (5/5)

This book deserves a prominent spot in bookstores, especially in sections for memoir, spirituality, nature writing, or elder wisdom. With its gentle pace and timeless themes, it appeals to a wide audience: from nature enthusiasts and spiritual seekers to caregivers, grandparents, and anyone reflecting on life's deeper meaning.

Having it available in physical stores invites serendipitous discovery, allowing browsers to flip through its pages and immediately connect with its beauty. Its thoughtful content also makes it a wonderful gift, a conversation starter, and a gentle companion through life's quieter seasons.

Moldwin has created something truly special, a work that reminds us that even the smallest leaf or deepest root holds a story worth listening to.

© **KSL PROFESSIONAL BOOK EVALUATOR**

K S Kravitz & Sons
INNOVATORS IN PUBLISHING, MARKETING AND ADVERTISING

A Community of One Hundred Trees and a Memoir of One Family Tree

To my wife, Sally; my parents, Mary and Bailey Moldwin; my daughter, Jennifer and her husband, John Gustafson; my son, Mark and his wife, Patty Hogan; and my youngest, Mara and her husband, Don Larsen. I owe them my deepest love and admiration and this book is dedicated to them.

My two-acre property and garden speak to the senses, palpable love songs of the heart. The wooded thicket, containing about a hundred species of trees, instills a sense of tranquility and harmony and showcases nature's unimaginable creativity. Living on Lake Huron, in the Thumb of Michigan, where the lake's ever-changing views— or moods?—inspire me, I ponder the concepts of simplicity, aging, growth, and time. As Luther said: "God writes the Gospel not in the Bible alone, but on trees, flowers, clouds, and the stars."

Since the mid 1970s, this small wooded thicket on the shoreline of Lake Huron has been my home and arbor. Before becoming a lakeshore retreat, farmers attempted to raise crops and graze their cattle on our property; in fact, I have unearthed old barbed wire fencing. Before the farmers, the land originally provided hunting grounds for various indigenous Americans, mainly the Chippewa/Ojibwe, Odawa and Potawatomi. In geologic history, as the glaciers receded from the Thumb and disappeared about ten thousand years ago, they accumulated thousands of feet of snow. The bottom parts turned to ice and the flows became a glacier about one mile thick! Melting and draining east to west from the apex of the Thumb (not south to north), the glacier left rivulets and deposits of rich loam and sand, where many species of trees took root.

My curiosity about trees, as an armchair or amateur botanist was peaked in New Britain, Connecticut, when I began to ponder my retirement. Not one epiphany, but many—rambling thoughts that sauntered up to me as I strolled around Walnut Hill Park near our house. The park was established in 1860 on about ninety acres, and I walked there often. I identified all its trees and even suggested other species to plant to the groundskeepers that I had gotten to know. I realized that humans and trees have the same requirements for existence: air (oxygen), light, warmth, water, and food. Greater awareness of trees began to grow within me as did the desire to learn their science and history. That is when I began to experiment with the cultivation of various species.

The Japanese would refer to my walks in the woods as "forest bathing." In the book, *Shinrin Yoku,* by Yoshifumi Miyazaki, 2018, he and other colleagues studied the physiological and psychological effects of nature, specifically forests, on human health and wellbeing. They concluded that forest bathing reduces stress, boosts your immune system, and decreases blood pressure as well as pulse rate, among other health benefits. To which I say, "Amen!" The American Osteopathic Association reported in their 2016 journal that about 72 percent of their patients are disconnected not only with nature or their environment, but also with family, friends and acquaintances at work. Richard Power in *Book Page* uses the term "species loneliness" to explain the psychology of loneliness, as most folks are alienated and crave friendship and intimacy. Talking or singing to trees may be a good idea for all of us! The more I know and remember, the more my relationship with trees deepens. Another favorite author of mine, Dr. Bernd Heinrich (b. 1940, biologist at the University of Vermont) in one of his award-winning books, *A Year in the Maine Woods*, indicates, "What we can't identify doesn't exist for us, … psychological possession of what we recognize; the more that you know, your relationship deepens."

I learned the poem "Trees" by Alfred Joyce Kilmer, 1886-1918, as a child:

> *I think that I shall never see*
> *A poem lovely as a tree[1]*

Of course, "Trees" is sing-songy and saccharine, inspiring many writers to parody it.[2] But every tree does evoke in me the same universal emotion of love embodied in the original verse. This book is my attempt to share my love of trees.

Countless volumes have been written on trees, but I felt compelled to tell my story—an exercise of personal, spiritual and scientific discovery. This book grew out of years of conversations with scores of master gardeners and assiduous reading of numerous books on trees and shrubs. Please email me for suggestions of which books to acquire and read.

-Bill
william.moldwin@frontier.com

---

[1] This poem, first published in the collection Trees and Other Poems in 1914, is in the public domain, and can be found here: https://www.poetryfoundation.org/poetrymagazine/poems/12744/trees

[2] One of the best-known parodies is "Song of the Open Road" by American humorist and poet Ogden Nash, in which he compares the trees in the poem to billboards.

And this our life, exempt from public haunts
Finds tongues in trees, books in the running brooks,
Sermons in stones, and good in everything.
       — Shakespeare, As You Like It

Contents

QUERCUS

The Oaks

My initial thought for the book was to begin by describing the wood used in the construction of our home. Upon retirement, I paid $660 for a contractor's license so I could build a house on our two-acre property to replace the original old concrete-floored cottage. Why not begin by recalling the stories of the exterior red cedar shingles, or the flooring—red oak "seconds" with its knots and various colors, giving it a rugged character? Now I'm pondering which tree or trees are my favorite. The choice of species changes every time I wander our wooded thicket. And the envelope please—for deciduous trees, the winner is the oaks! The poet John Evelyn begins the first chapter of his book *Sylva, or A Discourse of Forest-Trees and the Propagation of Timber in His Majesty's Dominions* by exclaiming: "What should move Pliny to make a whole chapter of one only line?" So, along such sentiments, I have sometimes considered writing only about oaks. But perhaps Pliny was right, as Evelyn continues: "The oak carries such a cargo of symbolism that embroidery is counter-productive."

And so I begin, first, with the etymology of the oak. Our English word oak comes from the Old English *ac*, related to the Dutch *eik* and German *eiche*. Scientific tree and plant names follow a pattern of separating name and description, a system established in 1753 by Swedish naturist, Linnaeus. He said a name should be in two parts only, the first word stating the genus (*e.g., Quercus*) and the second representing the species. For the English oak, he chose the Latin word *robur* meaning "strong" and so the binomial name *Quercus robur* was coined. I planted an English or Norman oak on the north side of the driveway, given to me by Jasper John, our grandson, after he returned from five years living in Germany.

The oaks, like all trees, grow from meristem tissue cells, which, dividing indefinitely, give rise to everything among and between the bark and the wood—*voila*—a tree. The tissue cells responsible for the widening of the tree are called the cambium; when forming *inward* toward the center, they become the xylem, or wood that transports water up the tree. Cambium tissue cells that form *outward* become the phloem which mainly is concerned with the transport of organic material down the tree – the glucose, starch, oils, and such made during photosynthesis. See *Miracle of Trees* by Olavi Huikari.

The xylem serves as a suction system and is four times stronger than the minimum strength needed to lift water. In other words, it can "lift" four times the water needed from the roots to the top of the tree, functioning as a perfect vacuum. On a warm day with water available, it can lift more than four gallons of water per hour through a single eight-inch diameter trunk. Think of the sugar maple tree in high spring—with optimal conditions, its sap can reach velocities of two hundred feet per hour, or better than three feet per minute.

It is often thought that a tree's branches and roots are mirror images of each other. To test this, extremely patient Scandinavians painstakingly scraped the soil to inspect the root systems of mature oak trees. They gave up when the distance of the root mass from the trunk was nearly three times as wide as the maximum spread of the tree's crown. Root hairs, almost microscopic in size, attract beneficial fungi to bring vital nutrients to the tree. An average mature red oak has more than five hundred million living root tips. Unlike leaves, these persistent roots grow continuously from March through October.

The oak's branching pattern is unusual. The lower limbs habitually descend in a graceful cascade effect like many conifers, whereas the higher limbs habitually ascend as a funnel reaching up to over 125-130 feet, reminiscent of the flowing currents of Lake Huron. In *Oak, the frame of civilization*, the author William B. Logan quotes the mystery writer Wilkie Collins, "Fancy and imagination, grace and beauty, all those qualities which are to the work of art what scent and beauty are to the flower, can only grow towards heaven by taking root in the earth."

The most critical building blocks for planting trees, and all plants, are the nutrients of soil. Soil, incorrectly called "dirt," contains billions of rock fragments of near-microscopic sizes of sand and loam from the decomposition of other organisms. Trees absorb water and a wide array of minerals from the soil to satisfy all the needs of photosynthesis and to counter water evaporation from the leaves. The minerals sought by roots include nitrates, potassium, phosphorous, iron, magnesium, calcium, and sulfur. Zinc, copper, and manganese are also found in healthy soils. Strange as it seems, roots need nitrogen in the greatest quantity but are unable to use atmospheric nitrogen, which comprises about 78 percent of the air we breathe. Instead, they take nitrogen from ammonia (NH_3) and nitrate (NO_3) compounds. The legions of soil bacteria convert atmospheric nitrogen to ammonia or nitrate. Different bacterium thrive in healthy soil with a near-neutral pH level. The pH level indicates whether a soil is acidic, neutral, or alkaline. Most oaks prefer neutral to slightly acidic soils where the necessary bacteria thrive. What I have seen in several books and have used in master gardener presentations to remember the macronutrients trees need is this easy-to-remember catchy rhyme: C HOPKN'S CaFe, Mg (mighty good!). Got it?[3]

Trees strongly influence the climate, and for the trees to help us maintain a planet in which we can thrive, we must maintain the quality of the soil—just ask any cash crop farmer. To this end, Sally and I maintain a compost pile to nourish our trees.

It is miraculous that the tree transforms warming light from the sun into chemical energy. When I imagine a mighty oak with a sturdy trunk, I think of the Bur oak in Ann Arbor, Michigan, and how it elevates its canopy above the competition. Yet despite its grand size, it is only able to photosynthesize about one percent of the sunlight it receives, and then only about ten percent of that one percent gets converted into wood—amazingly slow growth! Oaks can live up to six hundred years or more under the right conditions. One of the oldest white oak trees is in the churchyard of ivy-covered St. Paul Church at Fairlee, Maryland, planted in 1713. Its girth is over twenty-three feet and it stands at 118

---

[3] C (Carbon) H (Hydrogen) O (Oxygen) P (Phosphorus) K (Potassium) N (Nitrogen) S (Sulfur) Ca (Calcium) Fe (Iron) Mg (Magnesium)

feet with a spread of 127 feet.

The fantastic colors of trees throughout the year allow us to witness the different frequencies of light used by trees. The working cells of the leaves are chloroplasts which maintain a tree's life. They absorb light's red and blue wavelengths—around 700 and 450 nanometers respectively. (A nanometer is a billionth of a meter.) The unused green light (nanometers) is reflected back to us, indicating that the tree is alive and taking in the energy from the reds and blues.

Because summers are generally dry and hot, enzymes break up the green chlorophyll particles, reducing their use of red light and reflecting it instead. Only then can we see the other pigment that had been in the leaf all along, carotenoid, bursting forth the outstanding yellows, oranges and browns. We can mark the annual phenomena as the change of seasons with "color tours."

Other ultra-light spectrums are transported through the leaves before the leaves begin to fall. The way I recall this "color parade" is to remember that it is God's artwork, like rainbows, resulting in ART, wavelengths of absorption, reflection and transit, or simply transition.

Oaks often have many types and shapes of insect galls—woody or fruit-like, mossy or wooly, round or bunched. They occur on leaves and twigs and are visible in late summer and fall. Over eight hundred species of gall-makers live on oaks, and virtually all of them are a family of tiny wasps, the *cynipidae*. I see these quite often and yet still ponder, "'Are they beneficial or harmful?'"

Oak bark is tough and more robust than the smooth-skinned bark of beech, for example, and can withstand a lot of punishment. It's no skin off an old oak's back if a wild boar wants to use its bark as a scratching post!

Native Americans and settlers found many uses for oak acorns. After they leached the tannins from the acorns by soaking them in water, they roasted them for "coffee" and used ground acorns as a thickening for stew, or to make bread, pancakes, beer or mead.

Every majestic oak tree was once a
nut who stood its ground!

Oaks are mentioned at least twenty-six times in Biblical passages, depending on the translation. For example, Israelites were called "oaks of righteousness" (Isaiah 61); Abraham's oak is called the "Oak of Mamre" (Genesis 18); and Jacob buried foreign gods under the "Oak of Shechem" (Genesis 35). I cannot find any references to oaks or oak trees in the New Testament.

Historical and literary references to oaks are quite numerous. Many books have been written on each of the hundreds of oak species. Worldwide, oak species number about six hundred, of which about ninety grow in the United States, including hybridized shrubs.

> *During seminary, I spent the summer of 1958 in clinical training at the New Jersey State Psychiatric Hospital, Greystone Park, near Madison, New Jersey. I was tasked with developing oral weekly reports on patients for several psychiatrists and the chaplain, George Tolson. Each of the seven patients presented with different diagnoses, which allowed me to learn a bit about psychiatry. As a young man, I was also interested in exploring the relationships of my parents. I still recall my "analysis" of Dad, "permissive, but not submissive," and of Mom, "assertive, but not aggressive." The whole experience piqued my interest in mental health issues—which continues to this day.*

When my folks died, I planted a Hungarian oak for each of them because of their longevity and quiet strength and because I am Hungarian. My father was a Magyar from Cleveland, Ohio, *nee* Lovasy, and given the adopted name Moldovanyi from his stepfather, which was eventually shortened to Moldwin. My Dad was born on January 13, 1904 and died on February 27, 2000. My Mom, also a Hungarian from Cleveland, was born on September 9, 1911 and died on August 20, 2003. Ponder the fact that my folks, as well as all humans, share about fifty percent of our DNA with trees!

One of my favorites, "Song for My Father," composed, played and sung by Horace Silver aka Silva (1928-2014) honored my Dad's life at his funeral. Perhaps you can hear why I chose the oak to honor him and my mom.

If there was ever a man
Who was generous, gracious and good
That was my dad
The man
A human being so true[4]

Hungarian oak leaves are broad with short points colored with a light yellow-green that expands out into a rich beautiful dark green, offset with upward pointing hairs. Our two gorgeous trees are doing well and often catch an admiring eye.

> *Our graduate school, Hartford Theological Seminary, where Sally and I met, sponsored two Hungarian freedom fighters who escaped through the Austrian border before the Soviets put down the Hungarian revolution in the fall of 1956. Three of my cousins also joined the revolutionaries and lived to tell vivid and tragic stories. The Soviets invaded Hungary on November 4, 1956 to quell the "uprising," killing 1,519 civilians, imprisoning many, and deporting many others to Russia. Official reports indicate that 699 Soviet soldiers were killed by Hungarian organized soldiers, workers, and students. Two of those "workers" were housed in the seminary dorms and assigned to me as the manager or steward of the dining facilities. One gave me the arresting poem "Hunger" by Gyorgy (George) Gomori, which I appreciated.*

Over the years, I have casually distinguished black, red, and white oaks, but there are botanical distinctions. The white oak group is made up of eastern white oak (the king of the oaks), post oak, overcup oak, swamp white oak, chestnut oak, basket oak, Gambel and Chinquapin or Muehlenbergii oak (a dwarf Muehlenbergii oak thrives on the

---

[4] The composition "Song for My Father" was released by the Horace Silver Quintet on the Blue Note label in 1965. I encourage you to listen to the full lyrics from the song.

southside of our west walkway), and the Bur or mossycup oak (such as the mammoth oak at the School of Business, University of Michigan, Ann Arbor). Bur oaks grow along the westside of our property, adjacent to M-25.

The botanical distinction between white and red oaks is that white oak acorns form and fall in a single year and are reasonably sweet to eat; red oak acorns take two years to form on the tree and the meat is bitter. What survival strategies! I am still amazed even as I get to know the differences between the species. White oak has scaly whitish grey bark, in contrast to the blackish and furrowed trunks of the red oaks. The deep lobes of the white oak leaves are rounded at the ends, without the points or bristles of the red oak leaves.

In addition to those eight species, the red oak group consists of ten species: Northern red oak (one of which was planted in the circle of our driveway by our "six" children), Spanish oak, scarlet oak, Shumard oak, black oak, pin oak, Northern Jack oak, shingle oak, willow oak, and blackjack or scrub oak. Various books differ in the number of species—some sources state approximately 450 species worldwide with about fifty species in the United States and other sources put the number at six hundred species worldwide with ninety-five species in the United States.

The Chinquapin oak (*Quercus muehlenbergii*) is classified as a distinct species, with no subspecies currently recognized. Its scientific name honors Gotthilf Heinrich Ernst Muhlenberg (1753-1815), a Lutheran pastor and amateur botanist in Pennsylvania and namesake of Muhlenberg College, Pennsylvania.

I stumbled across another botanist/naturalist in the name of William Gambel (1823-1849). Since I planted the dwarf Muhlenberg oak, I planted a dwarf Gambel oak in the center of the courtyard to honor him as well. The tree's wood is hard and dense, and it reaches only four feet in height. Its branches are irregular and crooked, and its acorns are about one-third enclosed by a cap or cuple (cup). Both the Muhlenberg and Gambel dwarfs in the courtyard have beautiful glossy dark green leaves which turn orange and yellow during autumn.

The English oak, known for its "staunchness," for centuries, built the English navy and merchant marine fleet. And not to be outdone, the American fledging navy and merchant marine shipbuilders exclusively used the best hard wood around, the white (American) oak!

The immortal frigate USS Constitution, still commissioned today, has a gun deck, hull and keel of solid white oak. We have visited Mara and Don in Boston where we walked the deck of "Old Ironsides," built in 1797, still feeling her oaken strength where she rests in Boston Harbor.

Legend has it that the Round Table of King Arthur was made of English oak. Robin Hood and his men stashed the deer they poached in the hollow of an English oak in the Sherwood Forest. The Charter Oak was also an English oak. Unfortunately, it was lost to fire when, according to legend, school children boiled a kettle for tea inside its famous hollow.

In 2000, I was invited to write an article on the "grandson" of the original Charter Oak in the Connecticut newspaper *The Herald*. The detailed history of this Connecticut landmark, made famous under the colonial Governorship of Robert Treat (1683-1698), resounds down the corridors of Connecticut high schools and colleges. Perhaps you recall the movie *"Man for All Seasons"* which depicts Charles I, beheaded in 1649 during Oliver Cromwell's rule? It was his son, Charles II, when restored to the throne, who expressed interest in the colonies and demanded that the "Treaty" or charter granted in 1662 be returned! When the King's emissary, dispatched to the Colonies on October 31, 1687, demanded that the charter be revoked, the room suddenly went dark, presumably because a gust of wind blew out the candles. When light was restored, the charter was gone! Legend would have it that the purloined document was hidden in an oak and this tree became known as the Charter Oak. This mighty oak is the reason that Connecticut was the only one of the thirteen colonies to retain its original charter as the basis for the state's constitution.

And I wonder—who hid the charter in the oak?

Quercus macrocarpa
Bur or Mossycup Oak

The University of Michigan successfully moved and relocated a 250 plus year old Burr (alternate spelling) or mossycup oak tree, rather than cut it down during a $140 million expansion of the Ross School of Business. Students and faculty started a petition in 2014 to save the tree and donors reluctantly designated $400,000 from the $110 million endowment to fund the preservation of the legacy tree. Journalist Jeremy Allen tells the amazing story in The Ann Arbor News, from November 2015.

The University contracted with a firm from Texas, Environmental Design, which spent the summer of 2014 wrapping the tree's enormous root ball and placing metal pipes underneath it prior to the unearthing and transplantation. Paul Cox, vice president of the company, estimated that the tree would have a "70 to 80 percent survival chance following the transportation." The oak weighed approximately 700,000 pounds or 350 tons!

"I would've thought there might have been a certain amount of transplant shock ... but there have only been positive surprises," said the university's horticulturist Marvin Pettway. He and others monitored the tree from a lift bucket to examine if the leaf buds were properly swollen, which is an indication that new growth would continue through the spring. (My Bur oak seedling, planted in 2014, is doing quite well on the west side of our property.)

On moving day October 25, 2014, during the final stages of the undertaking, one of the large rubber air bladders holding up the tree burst! It became a projectile and went through the windshield of an occupied construction vehicle. Fortunately, no one was injured but the incident stalled the transplant work. Environmental Design and Walbridge, a sub-contracted company, investigated the cause of the burst and considered other potential problems that could arise. The investigation lasted for over a week and given the green light, the oak reached its final destination on November 4, 2014.

For their efforts in preserving the Bur oak, the University of Michigan Ground Services department received the 2015 International Society of Arboriculture Gold Leaf Award for Beautification. Marvin Pettway accepted the award at a ceremony in 2015 in Lansing.

Imagine, Bur oaks blanketed the Huron Valley in the 1760's when groves of oaks dominated the terrain, along with butternuts and walnuts, species not known along the Eastern Atlantic seaboard. A grand Bur oak suggested to pioneers a house of itself—for its mighty boughs can extend horizontally fifty, sixty, or even up to seventy feet.

The Bur oak has the largest acorns of all the oaks, with rugged and deep fringed cups, as well as the largest leaves of extraordinary texture and patterns. It is slow growing and may not reach productivity for fifty years, when our grandchildren will be able to then harvest the acorns. Think of the fun the great grandchildren will have!

At Sioux City, Iowa, the Council oak, a Bur oak, was about 150 years old when Lewis and Clark made their way up the Missouri and, according to legend, held council with many important Native American tribes beneath its boughs. To the best of my knowledge, it is still growing.

It is astonishing that trees such as the Bur oak can distribute the necessary chemical nutrients to the farthest parts of the organism, up over two hundred feet. The root system is almost a mirror image of what we see stretching towards the sky. What a miracle of perfect plumbing to take up the nutrients from the soil, dissolved in water, via astronomical numbers of minute root hairs, passing the nutrients literally cell by cell, throughout the entire tree. Someone once said that aerodynamically bumblebees should not be able to fly. The same can be said of trees. Structurally, their root systems should "not" be able to distribute nutrients! Incredibly they can conduct more water than is required to maintain cell turgidity and to promote photosynthesis, providing surplus moisture through continual transpiration of water vapor from stomata and the undersides of leaves and young shoots—truly amazing!

Quercus palustris
Pin Oak

Friends and visitors to our home occasionally notice that the oaks, particularly my pin oak, retain their leaves until spring. (The pin oak was given to me by Pastor Gary Johnson of St. Peter Lutheran Church, Battle Creek, Michigan in about 1974.) There are no deciduous pines, no evergreen maples, no deciduous spruce, no evergreen ash or lindens, no deciduous cedars or junipers, but oaks are both deciduous and evergreen! Live oaks are eternally green with cupped, waxy, stiff, and sharp-tipped leaves. When a few leaves do fall to the ground, usually pale yellow, they are quickly replaced by new growth. The name live oak comes from the fact that these oaks remain green and "live" throughout winter, when other oaks are dormant and leafless.

My pin oak also refuses to shed its leaves. Although it is not technically considered a live oak, the pin oak retains its dry, dead, withered, stiff, tan-brown leaves as the stalks are still growing. This phenomenon is called *marcescens*. Why does it retain its leaves until the spring?

Botanists have differing opinions. In winter, deciduous trees hold concentrations of carbon, hydrogen, and oxygen as well as nutrients, dissolved minerals absorbed by the root system and built up during growing season: potassium, calcium, sodium, magnesium, iron, nitrogen, phosphorus, sulfur, iron, boron manganese, zinc, copper, molybdenum, and other minerals found in lesser quantities.

When trees begin to shut down for winter, they scavenge those nutrients from the leaves, storing them in woody tissue until they will be used to develop new growth the following spring. Layers of cork cells close the microscopic "pipe-lines" or veins between twigs and leaves and eventually, yielding to gravity, wind, rain, and snow, the leaves fall to the ground. But why do the leaves of my pin oak wait until the spring?

Oaks, having acidic leaves, prefer acidic soil, but the leaves will not change the soil's pH levels unless they are mulched and worked into the soil. By falling in the spring, the leaves actually serve as a buffer against drastically changed soil conditions. When the leaves do get pushed off and drop, the oaks essentially are creating their own compost raising the pH level of the soil, making it more alkaline and less acidic. The pH scale ranges from 0-14, with a pH of seven as neutral. As the number decreases from 7, acidity gets higher; as the number increases from 7, alkalinity gets higher. Oaks demand very acidic soil with a pH level of 4.5 to 5.5, which affords them access to all the nutrients derived from the fallen spring leaves, especially iron.

Having leaves that do not fall until the spring also provides the oak an advantage over other trees in retaining moisture. The leaves can trap snow and keep moisture at the base of the tree. The marcescent foliage also protects new leaves, petiole (stalks), and twigs from being browsed by herbivores.

Floyd Swink, arborist at the Morton Arboretum in Lisle, Illinois (twenty-five miles west of Chicago) wryly claims that the wooden puppet Pinocchio was made from pin-oak-io!

Red Oak

After my lengthy hospitalization for lymphoma in 2018, our "six" kids, our three kids and their spouses, bought me a large red oak, about twelve to fourteen feet tall, which I planted with the help of Brian Patterson, a local nursery professional. I love the radiant colors of pines, spruces, maples...but I especially love the colors that emanate from red oaks. The red color in their leaves is the result of a metabolic disorder! Most leaves produce their own sunscreen, acidic anthocyanin, which blocks the ultraviolet rays from the sun and protects the leaves. But the red oak lacks the enzyme needed to break down the anthocyanin and rid the leaves of their red color, leaving the tree with red leaves.

Green means that the tree is alive and well and absorbing red and blue energy. Yellow and orange colors, revealed when the chlorophyll breaks down, give us the autumnal colors to enjoy. In early autumn another pigment, carotenoid, colors the leaves with more vivid yellows, oranges and browns.

Photosynthesis is the conversion of sun (light/energy). This chemical energy turns into living organisms or "raw materials," predominantly CO_2 and H_2O (carbon dioxide and water), leaving "end products" which include oxygen, carbohydrates, sucrose, glucose, and starch.

When Sally and I built our home in 2000-2001 and were pondering which species of wood we would have for our floors, we knew of only two sorts of oak, "white" and "red." Lumber suppliers classified the oaks as "white – heavier, stronger, and durable" and "red – weaker, coarser, and less resistant to decay." At that time, white oak was growing harder to come by and becoming more expensive. We chose red oak. Red oak is now more acceptable, with its lighter color and visible grain lines giving it "character" (but it is still a lot less expensive than white.) Red oak grows faster than white oak, which was thought to impact the wood's durability. But our red oak floors will last just as long as white oak, especially because Larry and Chad Hooper, our painters, applied three coats of preservatives! We enjoy the various colors and imperfections in our flooring, and I often remark: "Wow! Life isn't perfect either!"

Once, in Connecticut, a professor from Manchester Community College and I trekked along the Quinnipiac River in search of its boggy headwaters. We could see the acorns already sprouting on the white oaks. That was the first time I noted that white oak acorns mature in one growing season, but that red oak acorns do not mature until the end of the second growing season. *Why??*

In his book, *The Natural History of the Oak Tree,* David Streeter describes caterpillars that time their hatching to the emergence of moist pubescent oak leaves. If they hatch too early or too late, they starve. *What??*

One can never exhaust the wealth nor mystery of the oaks.

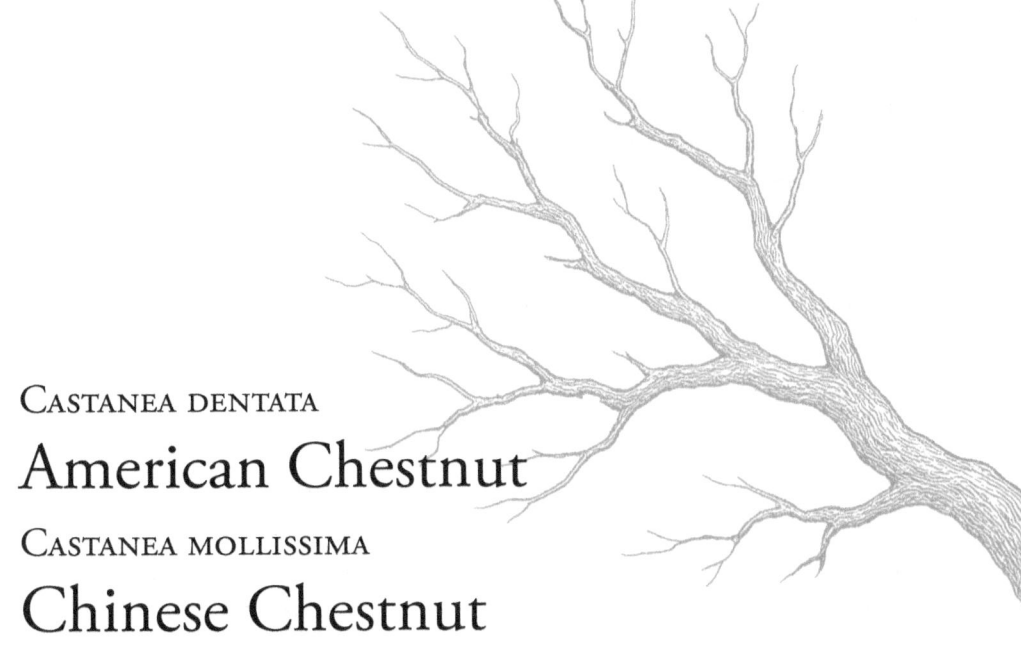

American Chestnut

Chinese Chestnut

The American chestnut once dominated the eastern part of the United States. Imagine squirrels clambering from chestnut tree to chestnut tree from Maine to Alabama without touching the ground! Chestnuts played a central role in the economy and culture of the Appalachian Mountains. Folks built their homes of chestnut logs, brewed home remedies from chestnut leaves, and roasted and sold the nuts to pay their taxes and buy or barter for necessities. Charlotte Ross of Appalachia State University, Boone, North Carolina, told members of the American Chestnut Foundation at their 2004 annual meeting: "If ever there was a place defined by a tree, it was Appalachia."

But have you ever seen an American chestnut tree? In the 19th century, Martin Hicks planted a handful of American chestnuts on his farm in West Salem, Wisconsin, which were given to him by his mother in Pennsylvania. Now the site hosts over 5,000 soaring straighttrunked trees, the largest stand of American chestnuts in the country. Sadly in 2005, the trees were infected with a fungus. Here's to hoping that blossom abundance, and the scientists working to try to save the trees, are successful so that the trees can continue to produce bushels of nuts for research.

All other major stands of American chestnut trees in the Eastern United States have fallen victim to a destructive plague and have died!

The cause was a fungus, *Cryphonectria parasitica*, formerly *Endothia parasitica,* that originated in China and surfaced in New York State in 1904. Known as chestnut blight, the fungus penetrates bark at the cracks found in crotches of limbs and lesions made by wood-boring beetles. The fungus then kills the entire cambium layer, eventually extruding its fruiting-bodies through the swollen and cracking bark, sending its spores from tree to tree by the wind. The disease was first noticed in the Brooklyn Zoo and quickly spread. Over the next fifty years, the blight killed over four billion trees and devastated communities that had come to rely on the chestnut tree for food, lumber and livelihoods. The remaining massive silvery carcasses and yawning stumps now "evoke an eerie feeling of longing for what must have been," as one American Chestnut Foundation member put it. One tree that managed to avoid infection with the blight due to its isolation, is in Grand Traverse, Michigan. It stands at 110 feet tall.

The blight may be inhibited if a biochemical peptide compound can be induced to form within the blight-susceptible trees via genetic engineering techniques. Molecular biologists are indeed attempting to introduce a gene which potentially could encode the trees with the capability to produce such a compound. The American Chestnut Foundation, located in Vermont, is producing trees that are 98 percent blight-resistant. How can we help reintroduce the American chestnut to its former range? Join one of the regional chapters of the foundation. I did, as did the women's organization WELCA (Women of the Evangelical Lutheran Church of America) at First Lutheran Church of the Reformation, New Britain, Connecticut, when I was pastor there.

Chestnut researchers are pursuing two other strategies: eliminate the fungus and hybridize the tree so the blight cannot damage it. I planted a hybridized chestnut, but it did not survive. Consequently, I planted three Chinese chestnuts and all three have produced edible nuts, delicious—reminding me of Nat King Cole's version of "The Christmas Song"!

In 1978, researchers in Europe discovered a naturally occurring virus that could "defang" or retard the fungus. Researchers, Italian and French, cultured samples and injected the strains of the "new" virus into the American chestnuts which dramatically slowed the growth of the original chestnut blight virus. Thus, the trees had time to marshal their natural defenses. This new phenomenon was called "hypo-virulence." Today, although those trees are riddled with blight cankers, they are still alive and continuing to grow.

We will have to wait and see if any of the newer hybrids take better advantage of hypo-virulence than others. As one plant pathologist said: "Some trees out there seem to 'get it,' and some of them don't." If you are ever near Meadowview, Virginia, visit the Chestnut Foundation Research Farm there. You can observe second generation hybrids that are methodically tracked to see how well each tree copes with the blight.

Fagus grandifolia

Beech

The beech, *Fagus grandifolia*, is a strikingly beautiful, tall, and stately tree. It is of interesting shape and has smooth gray bark. About 450 species of beech family (Fagaceae), both evergreen and deciduous, live in the temperate climates, including oaks, sweet chestnuts and beeches.

The beech's flowers appear after the leaves unfold, and both male and female flowers develop on the same tree. The male flowers appear as tight ball-like clusters; the female flowers are smaller and less tightly congested. The tree's fruits, or kernels, light brown and triangular-shaped, are borne in pairs of small, four-valved burs with recurved prickles. Beechnuts mature in October and drop during winter. Beechnuts are sweet, edible and nutritious, and provide food for deer, bear, raccoon, squirrels, grouse, wild turkey, and other wildlife.

Beech wood is close-grained, hard, strong, and tough. It is commonly used for flooring, cooperage, furniture, woodenware, and veneer. Beech bark has been used as writing paper for centuries. The word "book" comes from the Anglo-Saxon *boc* (letter), which derives from *beece* or beech.

The beech can obtain heights of sixty to seventy-five feet with diameters exceeding four feet. It has an unusually shallow root system and frequently sends up suckers from the roots. In autumn, the leaves first turn a rich golden yellow and then a coppery brown before they fall. Its trunk remains smooth, silvery and fresh-looking because, unlike other trees, it does not accumulate calloused cork-like bark as a protective layer. The beech's cambium stays almost on the surface.

If you were to carve your initials on the bark of a beech at eye level, as I have, you will discover over time that the scars of the inscription remain at the same level and spot even as the tree grows. If you do find a big beech tree, hacked by some love-struck boy with an outline of a heart and his girl's initials in it, forgive him! He is following a custom older than Shakespeare, who records the following:

O Rosalind! These trees shall be my books
And in their barks my thoughts I'll character;
That every eye which in this forest looks
Shall see thy virtue witness'd every where.
Run, run, Orlando; carve on every tree
The fair, the chaste and unexpressive she.

An old beech tree in Carrol Creek, Washington County, Tennessee, located on the stagecoach road between Blountsville and Jonesboro, bore this epic line for all those who passed that way since 1880 to see:

D. Boon CillED A. BAr on tree in the YEAR 1760

The tree fell in 1916 with the scars of the inscription still visible. The trunk of the Daniel Boone defiled beech is now on display in a museum in Louisville, Kentucky. It had reached a girth of twenty-eight and a half feet and a height of seventy feet tall when it fell, and was estimated to be 375 years old—which means that it began to grow in 1551, a half century before Orlando mooned about Rosalind in Arden! Let us not imitate the least admirable trait of Boone as we nurture and admire the tree planted on the north side of our driveway.

The virgin grandeur of this luminous tree once covered large parts of Ohio, Kentucky, Indiana and central Michigan. Pioneers believed that the beech was a sign of good soil—rich limestone overlaid by deep, dark loam. I marvel at the imagery contained in the 1833 writings of the German prince, Alexander Philipp Maximilian of Wied-Neuwied (1782-1867), an explorer ethnologist, naturalist and writer: "We came to a tall, gloomy forest which afforded a most refreshing shade. The forest continues without intermission, lofty crowns of the trees shut out the sun. The splendid forests constantly reminded us of the scenery of Germany." I imagine that they ate the beech nuts with a homesick sigh.

The beech tree—with its mast of edible nuts, stands as if a monument to past glories. It once was the predominant refuge of the passenger pigeon during migration. Flocks of millions were sustained *en route* by beech tree nuts until the last passenger pigeon died on September 1, 1914, in the Cincinnati Zoo.

Coincidently, as I research and write this chapter about the value of the beech tree and its importance, it is the birthday of John James Audubon. He was born on April 26, 1785 in Haiti, the son of a French merchant and a creole woman. He wrote the following:

> As soon as the pigeons discover a sufficiency of food to entice them to alight, they fly in circles, reviewing the country below. During their revolutions, the dense mass which they form exhibits a beautiful appearance, as it changes its direction, now a glistening sheet of azure, when the backs of the birds come simultaneously into view, and anon, suddenly presenting a mass of rich deep purple. They then pass lower, over the woods, and for a moment are lost among the foliage, but again emerge and are seen gliding aloft. They now alight, but the next moment, as if suddenly alarmed, they take to wing, producing by flapping of their wings a noise like the roar for distant thunder, and sweep through the forests to see if danger is near. Hunger, however, brings them to the ground. When alighted, they industriously throwing up the withered leaves in quest of the fallen mast.

Audubon was undoubtedly observing the layered canopy of mature beech trees, which lets only threads of sunlight through to the spaces below; any bird calls within returning the long-answering echo of an empty room.

Not everyone loves beech trees as much as I do. British botanist, Alan Mitchell (1922-1995), a passionate forester, dendrologist, and author once opined: "…they are anathema; heavy, dark masses, garish without being bright, blending with nothing, contrasting pleasantly with nothing, absorbing light uselessly." Of course, he is entitled to his opinion, but he is wrong! Ironically, I note that it was he who identified a serious bark-fungus disease introduced by beech scale insects from Europe.

ACER
The Maples

Varieties of maples, or *Acer*, abound. There are about one hundred species, including the exotic. They are all similar in that each has fruit composed of two separable samaras or keys, also known as "whirlybirds," consisting of nut-like laterally flattened carpels furnished with long, papery, tiny wings which broaden near the outer ends. The sugar maple, of course, is one of my favorite varieties. Its fall colors are a riot of yellows, richest crimson, tumultuous scarlet, and brilliant orange with an over painting of red.

And who does not appreciate pure maple syrup on pancakes or waffles? Sap is collected from the trees and boiled down to concentrate the sugar to make sweet, delicious syrup. We went to a neighbor's farm, the Lee's, for a "sugaring off" party where we witnessed this process. Depending on the method of tapping, the size of the tree, and the given season, anywhere from five to forty gallons of sap can be drawn yearly from each tree. But it takes about thirty-two gallons of sap to yield one gallon of syrup. Yes, a thirty-two to one ratio! It also takes lots of patience, especially because the length of the season, from nine to fifty seven days at the end of winter, is not predictable.

As early as 1663, the English chemist, Robert Boyle reported to his colleagues: "There is in some parts of New England a kind of tree, whose juice that weeps out its incisions, if it be permitted slowly exhale away the superfluous moisture, doth congeal into a sweet and saccharin substance, and the like was confirmed to me by the agent of the great and populous colony of Massachusetts."

Figures and paintings from *Sugar and Sugar-making*, by James McNair, are on display at the Field Museum of Natural History, Chicago.

Native Americans, having no metal vessels to endure direct contact with the fire, often let the sap freeze instead of boiling it. Taking off the ice from time to time would concentrate the syrup. Or they would boil it by dropping hot stones into sap troughs. They recognized that maple sugar and honey were wholesome "medications" in their diet. Now we know that maple syrup contains phosphates that promote calcium retention, leading to stronger bones.

Under general forest conditions, a sugar maple can grow 120 feet tall, with a three to four foot in diameter trunk. Larry Hooper and family have a tree of such size on their property in Deckerville. (Larry painted our newly built house in 2001.) To achieve its stature, their maple had to survive not only the logger's axe, but the fire of 1881 as well!

The Thumb Fire of 1881 burned over a million acres in less than a day. It was the direct consequence of drought, hurricane-force winds, and the ecological damage wrought by that era's farming and logging techniques. After cutting and clearing acres of woods, pulling the stumps and piling the wood along the fields, the farmers poured kerosene on the wood piles before lighting them and "letting it run." Little did they know, nor undoubtedly could they have imagined, the conflagration which would spread to consume most of Huron, Tuscola, Sanilac and Lapeer counties. The Thumb Fire killed 282 people and caused tens of millions of dollars of damage.

Jennifer gave us a sugar maple (*Acer saccharin*) sapling in 1988, just before we moved to New Britain, Connecticut. I planted it on the south side of our property near the side door amidst the lilac bushes.

Her husband John's grandfather, Elmer Theodore Gustafson, from Eastern Nebraska, fashioned the headboard in the guest bedroom on the lakeside of the house, from a single long and wide board of maple with a beautiful grain. I am guessing it to be a sugar maple because wise settlers planted hardwood maples along the boundary lines of their farms as a source of revenue.

Besides sugar maples, we have black, box, elder, plane, silver, red, and Japanese maples on our property. The *Acer japonica* tends to have more leaf lobes than other maples, from seven to 11, and is known for its deep-cut fan shaped leaves. Japanese maples grow in a variety of colors, with leaves ranging from lacey to quite rugged. They are hearty enough to survive our winters and can be found all around our property.

I planted a sapling, about two feet tall, which I had thought to be a red maple, but it may actually be a London Plane, *platanus*. I will have to wait for years for the fruit to develop to know for sure. Stay tuned.

I hate to admit it but I also planted an invasive species, a Norway maple, *Acer platanoides*, on the south side of our driveway. This begs the question—when does an immigrant or invasive species become a permanent resident? The Norway maple was introduced into the United States in 1756. I am intrigued by the way it oozes a milky sticky sap from the veins or petioles of the leaves if cut. Its leaves are yellow and brown depending on the season—not too shabby. Nurseries and tree farms do not, I repeat, do not, recommend planting the Norway maple because it displaces native trees, shrubs and herbaceous understory plants. Ugh!

Jennifer and John Gustafson have a marvelous striped or moosewood maple, *Acer pensylvanicum*. The tree has remarkable fall colors and is thriving.

When I was a child growing up at 944 Clinton Avenue, South Euclid, Ohio, our street was lined with great big silver maples, Acer saccharinum. The trees had massive roots, lots of seeds and a weak crown structure.

I marveled at the silver maples when, over the years, their roots lifted up and broke the slate sidewalks and split the poured sidewalks. Which is why we rode our bikes in the unpaved gravel streets! Silver maples were viewed as a "poor folk's tree" because we poor folk planted them in lieu of more expensive "quality" trees. I recall welcoming the aerial assault of ripe maple seeds as a harbinger of summer vacation!

When my folks built a new house right next door to the old one in 1961-62, they planted no trees in front of the house and one Crimson King Norway maple in the backyard, far from the septic tank, near where we had a Victory Garden and kept chickens during the second world war.

My friend and neighbor in Detroit, Dr. Leon Brown and his two sons, also planted a Crimson King Norway maple. They planted it on the west end of the Chateaufort Place parking lot in honor and memory of their wife and mother, Joyce, who died in 1996. Joyce loved the Norway maple because of its colors. Sally and I journeyed to Stratford, Ontario, with Leon and Joyce every summer for about thirty years to enjoy Shakespearian plays.

The red maple or *Acer rubrum*, is the most common maple in the Eastern United States. In New England in particular, the red maple is striking because of its early red flowers and fall color. It has a pyramidal shape and gray bark, and prefers soils with a pH factor above 7.0. The red maple generally grows up to forty to fifty feet tall with a trunk diameter of two to four feet. Although the national champion, located in St. Clair County, Michigan, is 179 feet tall and nearly six feet in diameter. It has shallowly lobed leaves, paired samaras with wings that are slightly divergent from each other with tips pointing outward, red buds, red petioles, and red flowers. It is the earliest to flower of the trees on our property.

The wood of the red maple is moderately heavy, soft, and neither strong nor durable. However, it can still be used for furniture, wooden wares, boxes, crates, pulp, and distillation products. Red maple is frequently planted as an ornamental or shade tree. Syrup can be drawn from it, although in smaller quantities than from the sugar maple. Pioneers and settlers made ink from the tannin of the tree's bark by adding sulphate of iron. Adding alum instead produces a cinnamon-colored dye.

John Josselyn (1608-1675) was an English writer who wrote three hundred books on the fine arts, forestry and religious topics. In *New England's Rarities Discovered*, 1672, he wrote: "The Natives draw Oyl, taking the rottenest maple wood, which burnt to ashes, they make a Lye therewith, wherein they boil their white oak acorns until the Oyl swim on the top in great quantities."

The red maple's bark can cause hemolytic anemia in horses, fatal in some cases, if horses develop a taste for it or for the tree's foliage. Is that why the settlers and farmers in the Thumb preferred oxen to plow their fields?

Scores of moth species feed as caterpillars on the foliage, and bees are needed to pollinate the flowers. Although canker fungus can develop within tiny wounds in the bark caused by egg-laying tree crickets, an infected tree, hopefully, will recover within a year.

The red maple tree is the state tree of Rhode Island. Rhode, a translation from Dutch, gives us "Red" as in Red Island; hence the state tree.

The Griggs "creek" or stream runs through our property from the bridge on M-25 angling southeast to the Marilyn Manor stream and then into Lake Huron. It flows continually throughout the year, draining over six hundred acres, but it is not spring fed as best as I can tell, having walked its length many times! Nonetheless, it creates boggy lowlands which nourish not only the white poplars, but also the ash-leaf maple (*Acer negundo*). The ash-leaf maple is a "three-flower" maple also known as the box-elder maple. It has pinnately compound leaves, taking their name from their feather-like appearance, which are distinguished by their coarsely toothed leaflets arranged along the middle vein. It is the only maple with bright green to green-purple branches. Its native habitats are the banks of bottomland streams and the margins of ponds and swamps. It is the least demanding of the maples, and several are growing in our woods. The tree grows rapidly and therefore its wood is light, soft, weak and close-grained. The tree can also contain small quantities of sugary sap, of good quality and taste.

When we bought our property in September 1977, Ed Buresh lived on Lakeshore Road north of us, on what he called the Griggs River. He shared the history of that "river" telling us that it used to meander through our property, eventually emptying into Lake Huron near Marilyn Manor. He told me that after World War II, when M-25 was paved and fishing cabins, cottages and retirement homes were built, the tributary was filled over with sand and soil to allow for driveways from

M-25 to the lakefront.

When we lived in New England for about twelve years, from 1988 to 2000, we arranged numerous fall bus tours with friends and members of the First Lutheran Church of the Reformation to observe the visual effect of sugar trapped in the dying leaves of maples displaying an infinity of fiery colors. New England has cold autumn nights coupled with sunny days, resulting in the most pyrotechnical palette of anywhere on earth! We were corny "leaf-peepers," photographing the far-reaching canopies of red, gold, yellow-green leaves throughout the six states.

In 2001, Barry Bonds, born in 1964, had swapped his traditional ash bat for a maple bat when he hit the most home runs in a single season, seventy-three. Go figure. He was accused of using performance enhancing drugs and was indicted in 2007, but perjury charges were dropped in 2015.

On a lighter note, pun intended, one of my favorite songs from the American songbook is "Autumn Leaves," which I believe refers to a red and gold sugar maple mentioned in verses by French poet Jacques Prevert in "Les Feuilles Mortes" or "Dead Leaves." The musical setting of the song is by Hungarian composer, Joseph Kosma, and the English text is from lyricist Johnny Mercer. This elegy to heartache has had quite an odyssey since 1955, when pianist Roger Williams's cascading piano effects turned it into a million-record selling hit that is still popular today.

The poet James Russell Lowell (1819-1891), Boston, Massachusetts, with origins back to the Mayflower, penned this familiar poem, "The Maple":

The maple puts her corals on in May,
While loitering frosts about the lowlands cling,
To be in tune with what the robins sing,
Plastering new log huts 'mid her branches grey;
But when thee autumn southward turns away,

Then in her veins burns most the blood of spring,
And every leaf, intensely blossoming,
Makes the year's sunset pale the set of day.

John Muir (1838-1918), founder of the Sierra Club and known as the "Father of National Parks," penned stories about maples, saying "No finer forest ceiling is to be found than these maple arches."

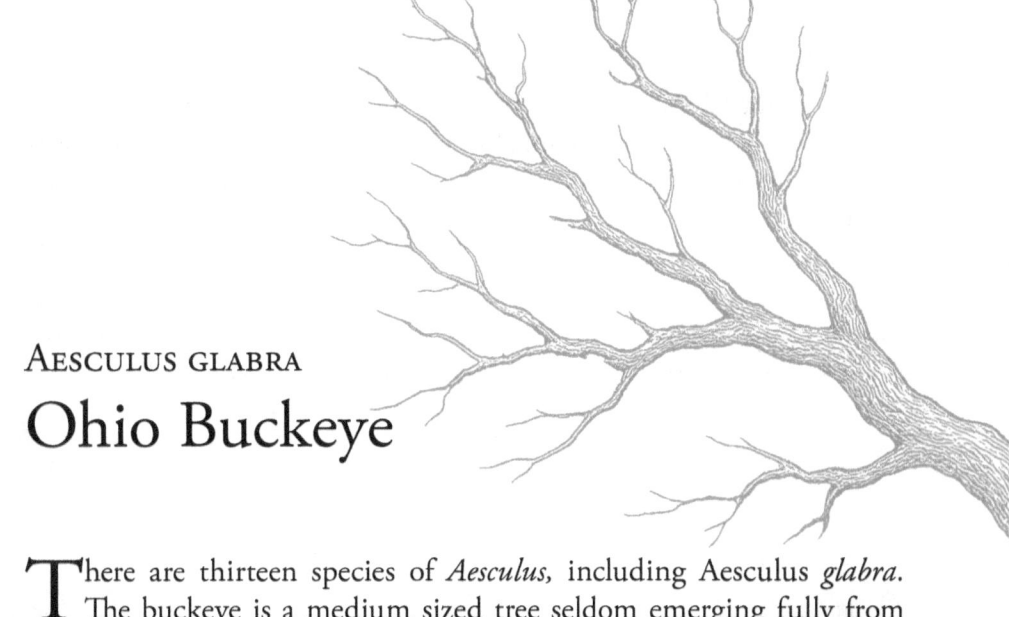

Ohio Buckeye

There are thirteen species of *Aesculus,* including Aesculus *glabra.* The buckeye is a medium sized tree seldom emerging fully from the shade of its taller acquaintances, like oaks. It is typically found growing in rich stream valleys. The buckeye is the state tree of Ohio, my birthplace, although the tallest "Ohio" buckeye is across the stateline in Liberty, Kentucky, standing 144 feet tall with a trunk about three feet in diameter. Buckeyes are distinguished by showy flowers in pyramidal clusters, large handsome foliage, spiny husks, and having large winter buds. Several beautiful buckeyes are thriving on our northern property line east of the garage.

The name "buckeye" is traceable to the brown nut marked with white, recalling the eye of a deer. Native Americans called them *hetuck* meaning "buckeye." Its cousin, the horse chestnut, employs the word "horse" to indicate that the fruit is inedible—neither are fit for human consumption. I have tasted a buckeye and it is foul, rank, and bitter. No wonder even the squirrels won't eat them! The highly toxic substance in the nut is aesculin. When food sources were low, Native Americans would leach the buckeyes, boiling, peeling and soaking the nuts to rid them of the aesculin and make them edible. Apparently in England the buckeye is called a "conker." I know that children in Ohio have also adopted this name and are known to hide them in pockets and pelt unsuspecting friends as they walk to school!

The Ohio buckeye's wood is light, soft, and weak. It can be used for furniture, artificial limbs, woodenware boxes and crates. The tree is rarely planted as an ornamental tree. Although, since I am a buckeye, I planted a bottlebrush buckeye near our ancient apple tree. I appreciate its flowers and colors, and named it Michaux after the French botanist/explorer Andre Michaux (1746-1813). Michaux travelled on horseback through Ohio in the summer in 1785 and apparently remarked on the beauty of the tree. My "Michaux" stands about ten to twelve feet tall and has beautifully elongated inflorescences with numerous white flowers in spring. Quite unique when its blossoms and the apple blossoms emerge at the same time. In autumn, its leaves turn bright golden yellow.

AESCULUS HIPPOCASTANUM
Horse Chestnut

The Aesculus *hippocastanum* was introduced to the United States in Elizabethan times as an ornamental flowering tree. This fast-growing tree originated in the Baltic Peninsula, Greece, Albania and Macedonia. Hippocastanum means horse chestnut: *hippo* in Greek for "horse" and *castanum* meaning "chestnut." Not only does it grow fast, but it also grows *old*. The oldest dated tree in Britain was planted in 1664, over 350 years ago. Hard telling how long it will live, not knowing! Horse chestnut trees can grow to about seventy to eighty feet tall. Because of their fast growth, they tend to be symmetrically shaped and are excellent shade trees with their large leaves. They make for an interesting specimen for any home or garden.

The horse chestnut's sticky buds distinguish it from buckeyes. And as for design, its tall candle flowers have no competitors. Because of its tapering flame-like panicles, the tree is said to be "in candle" when it flowers. Each blossom has dashes of red and yellow in its throat, and the curving, yellow stamens thrust out forming the ruffled border of the corolla. If these candle flowers were rare, they would be as admired as orchids. Each candle cluster holds one shiny inedible fruit, or conker. Similar to the buckeye, the fruits contain poisonous glucosides which should never be eaten. Even the tree's young shoots and leaves will fatally poison livestock if ingested. Never confuse the horse chestnut with the edible nuts of the true chestnut (*Castanea*). Despite the toxicity of the fruits, an extract with medical uses as a skin protectant, known as "esculin," is obtained from the bark --go figure!

I planted a horse chestnut in the thicket near M-25. It is thriving. I enjoy the boldness of its design with its huge fingered leaves. Its dark foliage contrasts beautifully with its clusters of large red, pink and white flowers in the spring. In autumn, its leaves yellow and drop early without any splash of color.

Wood-carvers and turners like to use the tree's wood because of its unusual grain. Superstitious people believe that the tree's nuts can cure rheumatism if carried in one's pockets or purses.

Henry Wadsworth Longfellow's "spreading chestnut tree" in the poem, "The Village Blacksmith," was, in fact, a horse chestnut. He called the tree by its popular name in England, which left off the word "horse." Longfellow (1807-1882) was born in Portland, Maine (when it was still a part of Massachusetts), and later become professor at Bowdoin College, Brunswick, Maine. His well-known poems include "Paul Revere's Ride," "Evangeline," and "Song of Hiawatha." He penned "The Village Blacksmith" in 1842, which begins as follows:

> Under a spreading chestnut-tree
> The village smithy stands;
> The smith, a mighty man is he,
> With large and sinewy hands;
> And the muscles of his brawny arms
> Are strong as iron bands.

And which concludes as follows:

> Thanks, thanks to thee my worthy friend,
> For the lesson thou hast taught!
> Thus at the flaming forge of life
> Our fortunes must be wrought;
> Thus on its sounding anvil shaped
> Each burning deed and thought.

Well done I say to my favorite friend and poet!

A horse chestnut grew outside the 17th century canal house in Amsterdam, where the German born diarist Anne Frank and her family hid from the Nazis during the Second World War. Anne Frank wrote several times about this tree in her diary. It was the inspiration for "The Anne Frank Tree," planted in her memory and honor after the war. Since the turn of the century, the tree suffered from a bleeding canker disease and was condemned to be cut down in 2007. Although the tree was saved by a court injunction fought for by residents and the charitable foundation formed to protect it, a cruel storm toppled the entire tree in 2010. The foundation saved nuts from the tree and sent them to different arboretums. Here in the United States, eleven saplings were raised, and were distributed to various Holocaust remembrance centers, parks, museums and schools for planting.

Juglans nigra
Black Walnut

Walnut trees grow throughout Europe and Asia, although the walnut trees in Turkey and Kyrgyzstan are of a Persian variety, producing milder flavored nuts than the European variety. The ancient Greeks and the Romans cultivated walnut tree orchards and forbade their slaves to eat the nuts as it made them "shrewd and rebellious," according to Nancy Hugo in her book, *Seeing Trees*, 2011.

A unique feature of black walnut trees is the way their leaves emerge from pale grey twigs with a red tinge, sending off a sweet spicy smell, just after the male catkins develop. The female catkins are very tiny. The stigma, or pollen-receiving part of the female flower pistil, develops flowers and fruit as large as billiard balls. The male trees release their pollen, promoting cross-pollination with other walnut trees. It's a marvel that these trees are so reproductive and remain so throughout their lifespan, even up to 150-400 years. At that age, a black walnut's girth can be as large as two to six feet in diameter.

Walnut trees exude a poisonous (toxic) chemical called juglone, an allopathic quinone, from their leaves, bark, and fruit, which gets released into the soil. The trees secrete this brown-staining substance as a survival strategy, inhibiting growth of plants and trees within root range. Several authors maintain that the juglone also inhibits mosquitoes. I cannot attest to this fact—the lack of mosquitoes near my walnut tree might be because we have bat houses on our garage and four to six bats usually arrive each year from Kentucky caves.

Some familiar uses of black walnut are to make gunstocks and to render oils used for dyeing and tanning. But black walnut wood is especially popular to use for furniture. President Andrew Jackson had a hand-crafted black walnut desk, also called a secretary, in his home, the "Hermitage" in Nashville. For our marriage on June 4, 1960, my folks bought us a bedroom set comprised of a bed, two dressers and a large mirror crafted from beautifully grained walnut wood. I recall my Dad saying: "It'll last forever."

Knowing the value of the trees, colonists exported them to England from Virginia as early as 1610, predating the first slave ship to arrive in the colonies in 1619. Twenty nineteen was the four hundred-year commemoration of the initial slave ship sent to Virginia, which has been recently exhumed and restored.

The medicinal uses of walnuts have included the treatment of parasitic worms, infections, diphtheria, syphilis and leukemia, all with dubious clinical trials. Although according to the University of Louisville's Christine Lee Brown Environmental Institute, growing and eating walnut leads to several positive outcomes including longer life spans, lower levels of stress and lower rates of cardiac disease.

> *In the Fall of 1977, when we were members of Christ Lutheran Church, located at Third and Philadelphia in Detroit, a friend from the church, Leo Wessinger gave me a half-filled burlap bag of black walnuts. After scarification, I planted the dozen or so walnuts in mounds of two nuts each, thinking that I would cull out the weaker seedlings. All "six" saplings grew!*
>
> *About seven or eight years later, I was thrilled. One of the black walnut trees started producing walnuts! I ran to the "cottage" to inform Sally and then grabbed a plastic bag to gather them up, about eighteen or so. I set the bag under the tree, eager to inspect our other trees as was, and still is, my habit. About an hour later I came back to pick up the plastic bag of walnuts and it was totally empty- nary a one! As I looked around, gray and brown squirrels were snickering and chattering over their good fortune.*

Shelling black walnuts is not as easy as it seems, even after they have been drying in storage for the winter to be eaten the next spring. Using a hammer crushes the nut as well as the shell, so …the secret is to strike them over a stone with a larger stone so you can sample a mouthful of protein with no cholesterol. I have read that if you remove the husk while it's green, then dry the nut for two to three weeks, you will get a better tasting walnut.

For the trivia buff, the walnut is the official state nut of Missouri; pecan is the official state nut for Alabama, Arkansas and Texas; and hazelnut is the official state nut of Oregon which grows about 98 percent of all the hazelnuts produced in the United States

Butternut Tree

The butternut tree, also known as a "white walnut," is a unique species related to walnuts and hickories. It has a round-topped crown, produces sweet nuts, and has a mature height of forty to sixty feet. It typically lives only seventy-five to eighty years. The United States champion growing in Chester, Connecticut stands seventy-eight feet tall with a trunk nearly seven feet thick.

The butternut is monoecious, meaning it has male (stamina) and female (pistillate) flowers on the same tree, rather than perfect flowers. The catkins, composed of male flowers, droop and the female flowers, which grow in erect clusters, are wind pollinated. The twigs of the leaves are distinct. Look for the "camel face" of the leaf scars. A fuzzy brow surmounts the U-shaped groups of bundle scars, resembling the eyes and happy-face smile of a camel. The predominant bud, appearing just above the "eyes," will produce a leafy shoot the next spring. When torn, the leaves ooze a waxy, aromatic sap, the allopath juglone. The green parts of the tree wear a downy, velvet-like coat of fuzzy hairs.

Butternuts are edible and sweet. Their high oil content makes them naturally nutrient rich, and the settlers and pioneers enjoyed eating them. Native Americans would even cultivate them. The nuts were eaten raw or cooked and could be ground into meal or mixed with venison and bear meat. The Iroquois extracted oil from the nuts to use not only for cooking but for hair dressing. The butternut can also be tapped for its sweet sap, to be boiled down for syrup. The nuts can also be "pickled," which apparently can be served as a delectable relish with meat dishes. To which I say: "No thank you." (The butternut is also known for its laxative properties.)

One October, tempted by the smell of those juicy brown husks, I cracked open some green nuts on a convenient stone, and then wiped my fingers ineffectually in the grass. The stains eventually did wash away, but my memories are indelible! Now I understand how the Shakers of Lebanon, Massachusetts, learned to make a rich purple dye by boiling the husks along with the nuts. They then used it to dye wool cloth. During the Civil War, just the root bark of the butternut was used by backwoods regiments to dye uniforms, the nuts being saved for food. The tree's twigs and husks were boiled down to make a brownish yellow dye used to color homespun clothing. The "khaki" color of the uniforms is why the soldiers were called "butternuts" during the Civil War.

Because the butternut is vulnerable to fungus infection and *Melanconis* cankers, which progressively kill its branches, it is rarely recommended by landscapers for planting.

Butternut is a weak wood, but it has a splendidly figured fine grain, making it exceptional to use as interior paneling. Because of this quality, it held an elite status among wood carvers and was often used for carriages, cabinet work, and altars. Hopefully its status and importance will rise again among artisans and botanists of today.

A specimen still stands at the Bellaire Motel and Lodge, currently owned by Bill Douras at 120 South Ridge Road, Port Sanilac, Michigan. When we were building our house in 2000-01, I travelled to the Thumb from Connecticut monthly, and stayed with Bill's mother, Mrs. Diana *nee* Pagonis Douras. She and her husband planted the butternut tree near the driveway when they bought the Lodge years ago. My butternut came from the seeds of their tree. Other specimens that I have personally admired are in Stratford, Ontario on the grounds of the Shakespearean Festival.

There are also several butternut trees and black walnut trees on the property of the Sanilac County Historic Village and Museum. I served on the Board of Directors of the museum for ten years, as treasurer for two, and also established its foundation. The museum sits on seven acres of land acquired in 1964 from Captain Stanley Loop (1884-1977). Captain Loop's father, Dr. Joseph Miller Loop (1811-1903), built their home, a Victorian mansion with twenty rooms, in 1875-78, for $11,000. Captain Loop planted the trees.

In 2015, I was asked by the Sanilac County master gardeners to write an article for the local paper. I wrote a piece entitled "A Tree Is a Lovesong" about the butternut tree on French Line Road, about one and one quarter miles west of M-25 on the south side. The tree is stupendous in all its glory. I actually measured it and could not believe my own numbers—girth (circumference) at 54 inches chest high (give or take six inches because I was stumbling over the deep fissures made by the roots) is 162 inches or 13.5 feet, making the diameter (162 inches divided by Π or 3.14) 51.6 inches or 4.3 feet! If you get the opportunity, drive by and doff your hat. Or better yet, plant a butternut tree.

This uniquely American tree with its precious grained-wood is rapidly becoming scarce. The future does not promise better things unless its glory be restored by a planned forestry initiative and master gardeners.

CARYA OVATA

Shagbark Hickory

CARYA ILLINOINENSIS

Pecan Tree

Native to North America, the hickory derives its name from the Algonquin word *pohickery*. The word was first used in English by John Smith (1580-1631), with the spelling "powchickora," although the colonists of the Jamestown Colony apparently spelled it seventeen different ways. The Scottish botanist, Philip Miller (1691-1771), curator of Chelsea Physic Garden, christened the hickory with a separate name altogether, *Carya*. Carya is a Latin word derived from the Greek word *karya*, meaning "nut." Today, the shagbark hickory is also known as the shell-bark or scaly-bark hickory, or the upland hickory. A mature hickory can reach a height of fifty to eighty feet, with a trunk diameter of one to three feet.

Shagbark hickory is the northernmost and one of the most widespread hickories. The record specimen is located in the Sumter National Forest in South Carolina and stands at 153 feet tall with a diameter of three feet at chest height. The hickory tree is monoecious, having male catkins and small wind-pollinated female spikes which appear after the leaves unfold. Its leaves turn yellowish gold in autumn. Hickories grow very slowly and can live for two to three hundred years, given the right soil and weather conditions. They begin flowering and developing nuts at about age twenty. Thereafter, hickories produce nuts abundantly but only at about three-year intervals. So do not fret over a minimal crop in any given year, it is not unusual.

Native Americans ground and cooked hickory nuts with cornmeal, then baked them into small cakes. They tapped the trees, like maples, producing small quantities of sap for a tasty syrup. William Bartram (1739-1823), a naturalist and author, in *Travels in North America*, wrote: "The fruit is in great estimation with the Indians. The Creeks store hickory nuts in their towns as I have seen an hundred bushels of these nuts belonging to one family. They pound them to pieces and then cast them into boiling water, which, after passing through fine strainers, preserves the most oil part of the liquid; this they call by a name which signifies milk; it is a sweet and rich as fresh cream, and is an ingredient in most of their cookery especially hominy and corn cakes."

The wood is also favored for use when smoking meats; who has not tasted the hickory-smoked flavor of ribs?

The shagbark hickory is a symbol of pioneer history. With its hard sinewy limbs and rugged-shaggy coat of exfoliating bark, it mimics the pioneers in their fringed deerskin hunting shirts. Some have speculated that the tree's ornamental, exfoliating bark evolved as a deterrent to squirrels, but its gray, peeling, disheveled look is to no avail. The hickory nut is always quickly devoured by wood ducks, wild turkeys, chipmunks, fox, and of course, squirrels. Squirrels actually extend the forest by burying the nuts, serving as the species' principal dispersal agents. The tree's wealth of sweet, nutritious nuts is not only for wildlife, it often stood between pioneers and famine as they travelled into new regions of North America.

In the pioneer mind, the hickory was also a symbol of strength, and the nickname "Old Hickory" given to General Andrew Jackson (1804-1845), was a testament to his fortitude. During the War of 1812, the Secretary of War callously ordered Jackson to discharge his troops at Natchez, five hundred miles from home. Flatly refusing, he marched his men back along the Natchez Trail to Tennessee in order that they might be mustered out closer to home. Jackson shared the privations of his men, even sleeping with them on the ground, and thereby won their admiration: "He's tough as hickory." When he entered the White House as president, the crowds chanted the nickname that he had been dubbed, "Old Hickory." Jackson is buried beneath six towering shagbarks in the Hermitage Garden near his Greek Revival mansion in Nashville, Tennessee.

Hickory wood is hard, strong, and elastic, making it suitable for making sporting equipment, tool handles, ladders, gunstocks, and furniture. Native Americans used hickory wood for hunting bows.

The fuel value of shagbark is higher than that of any wood except locust. A cord of hickory is almost the equivalent in thermal units as a ton of anthracite (hard coal), and costs significantly less.

Unfortunately, shagbark hickory trees are not widely available for gardeners and arborists because they are hard to propagate, and transplant poorly. That is why I planted a *Hicoria* pecan (*Carya illinoisensis*) near the shagbark hickory tree growing on our property, and not another shagbark. The *Hicoria* pecan is less dense and faster growing than the shagbark hickory, but distinguished nonetheless. Both are thriving. The name "pecan" was given to the variety by Native Americans, who supplemented their diets with the small nuts. Who doesn't love pecans?

The Spanish explorer, Hernando de Soto (1500-1542), known for his conquest of the Inca Empire in Peru, was searching for gold in what is now considered the Southwest, when he crossed the Mississippi River and explored the swamps of Arkansas. When he emerged upon high dry ground, he found abundant nut trees, which he assumed were walnuts. They were actually pecan trees. In consequence, pecans were first known in the east as "Mississippi nuts," or "Illinois nuts."

Chroniclers of French Louisiana mention the pecan, telling us that Native Americans and Creoles appreciated the confection known as New Orleans praline. The first pecan cultivar (a plant variety that has been produced in cultivation by selective breeding) "Centennial" was propagated in 1848 by a Louisiana slave named Antoine, owned by J.T Roman. Roman owned 112 slaves, ninety-three of them field laborers. At thirty-eight years old, Antoine became known as a master gardener of plants. Because of his talents, he was valued at $1,000, an impossible sum at that time. Since "Centennial," more than five hundred varieties, from dozens of cultivars, have been propagated. Most modern-day orchards plant several different varieties, relying on cross-pollination to prevent scab diseases.

During the Great Depression, my Dad worked for the PWA, the Public Works Administration, which was part of FDR's New Deal. I recall him sharing stories about his work. He complained that dams they were building for the government raised the water levels, even behind levees, and were "drowning out all the trees, including hardwoods." I wonder how many pecan trees were drowned in Arkansas, Louisiana, and Texas.

The pecan tree is the state tree of Texas. It can reach a height of 120 feet with a circumference of about thirty feet, making it the largest of the native hickories. The tree will often live for three hundred years.

Please plant a hickory, or any of its many cultivars—mocker-nut, pignut hickory or a pecan—for posterity!

Witch Hazel

The witch hazel is an understory tree whose faintly fragrant flowers venture forth only when its dull yellow leaves have dropped and the autumn airs begin to chill. This unique native shrub has edible nuts, sweet kernels encased in "helmeted" fringed bracts. A true delicacy if you love nuts. The tree has twisted branches and crinkled leaves of pale greenish gold. Its fruits are stranger still. The fruits are small pods. The previous year's fruits ripen only when the current year's flowers open. When this happens, the pods explode open, scattering their little black seeds, about the size of BB pellets. The seeds are ejected with considerable force and can land several yards away from where the pods burst. When the pods are opening, if you put them into a paper bag, you can hear them pop like a popcorn popper.

Philologists dispute the origin or source of the name "wych hazel." Perhaps the name comes from the Anglo-Saxon *wicken*, meaning "to bend," or the Old English *wick*, meaning "quick" or "living," or maybe a more modern word, "switch". According to Julia Rogers in Volume Nine of *The Tree Book*, published in 1916: "A witch in old days was a person who did or said things not conventional. Our witch hazel has defied the ancient laws of the calendar—a very dreadful thing! So, it comes honestly by its name ... and refers to the sprawling habit of the tree. Surely the observer cannot miss seeing the little wizen witch faces grinning at him from all possible angles of the tree, their yellow cap strings flying in the wind, as if in defiance of the rumor that the days of witchcraft are past."

The name also could possibly come from the use of "water witches." Have you heard of the practice of not even thinking about digging a well until a divining rod pointed to a hidden spring? Mining regions of both England and the Appalachian states would also use a "hazel wand" to try and determine where the rich lines of coal or metal were before sinking a shaft. A divining rod was made by taking a forked branch of witch hazel, one whose points grew north and south, meaning it had felt the influence of the sun at its rising and setting. The wand would be carried with a point in each hand, leaving the stem to point forward. As superstition would have it, the stem would point to the ground when over coal or metal.

The astringent witch hazel water, or Hamamelis water, comes from the tree. It is prepared by steaming and distilling the tree's leaves, bark, and twigs. It is a clear and colorless liquid useful to clean skin. Julia Rogers asserted that in the late 19th century "every country and city drug store" sold Hamamelis water in a variety of brands, made from pure extracts of witch hazel.

Corylus avellana "Contorta"
Filbert Tree

Do not confuse the witch hazel tree with the *Corylus avellana* *"Contorta"* aka European filbert, twisted hazelnut, or cobnut. I have done so! But they are each distinct species altogether. The hazelnut is in the birch family and is native to Europe, Western Asia and Northern Africa. It grows in thickets, clearings and along streams. Its epithet *avellana* comes from the ancient city Avella Veccia (southern Italy, near Naples) where the filbert tree was cultivated by the Romans for their commercial edible roasted nuts. *"Contorta"* was discovered in an English hedgerow in the 1850's by Victorian gardener Canon Ellacombe.

Harry Lauder also called his walking stick *"Contorta."* Harry Lauder (1870-1950) was a Scottish tenor and comedian who performed in vaudevillian theatre using a cane, or cromach, made from filbert wood, as a prop, like Groucho Marx and his cigar. Lauder was the highest paid performer in the world in 1911 when he sold over one million records. He entertained troops during the First World War and helped raise funds for the troops and veterans (like Bob Hope during the Second World War and Vietnam). By 1928, the number of records he sold reached over two million. I enjoy listening to his act "Roamin' in the Gloamin'."

"Contorta" trees are monoecious, and their blooms appear on bare branches in late winter and spring before the leaves emerge. Their nuts are known as "cobnuts" and appear in terminal clusters of one to four nuts, half covered in ragged husks. The husk surrounding the nut extends beyond the nut by at least one inch to form a beak. The fruits

ripen in August and September. I believe that this dwarf tree deserves a more prominent place in landscapes and gardens for its historical significance as well as its unique beauty. I planted a *"contorta"* under our southern bathroom window in 2004 and it is thriving, sheltered from the wind off the lake.

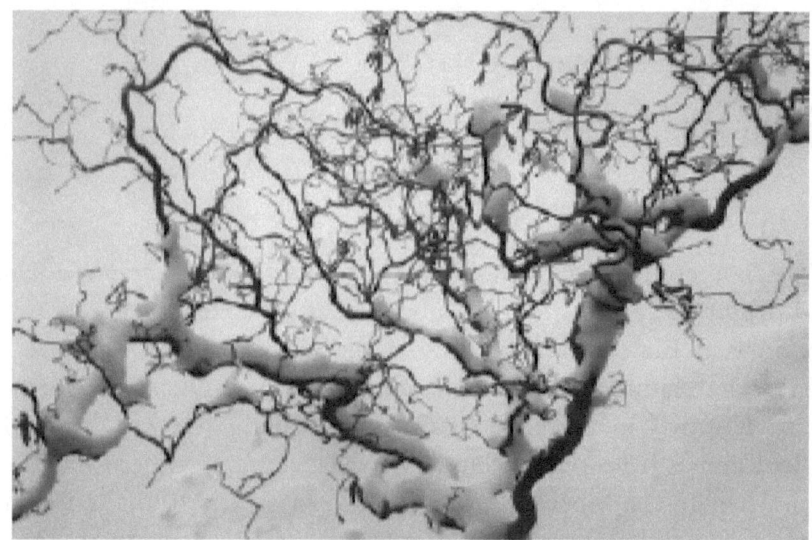

CORYLUS avellana "Contorta"

Cornus florida
Dogwood

The dogwood is a very well-known, beautiful genus of deciduous small trees comprising about thirty species. It is native to intemperate parts of the Northern Hemisphere. The name *cornus* (from *cornu*, a "horn"), references the toughness of the tree's wood. The dogwood's flowers are large and often showy. Botanists point out that the four white "petals" are not true petals, but bracts that make a clear and pleasing design alone or in mass. John Ray (1686-1704) was the first horticultural writer to highlight its ornamental qualities in *Historia Planetarium*.

The dogwood grows slowly into a multi-layered pagoda of color. Its symmetrical branching pattern gives it a sympodial crown of horizontal tiers. The trees bloom after about six years, producing an abundant seed crop every other year after that. The bark and branches remain vividly colored through the winter. In late summer, its red, blue or black berries attract many varieties of birds, including flycatchers, gray catbirds, yellow warblers, and American goldfinches. Although moth caterpillars, sawflies, beetles, and even fungus and cankers can attack dogwoods, causing infections and blight, to my knowledge they will not kill the tree. I have planted three dogwood saplings in the semi-shaded west-end thicket, but they are struggling to bloom as they demand full sun.

A canopy of understory dogwoods, with their supple, wispy stems, can reach about forty feet in breadth. The largest known tree, as of 2004, is an old flowering tree in North Carolina that stands thirty-one feet tall with a trunk about three feet thick.

The flowering dogwood is the state tree of Virginia, Missouri and North Carolina. George Washington, an inveterate planter of shrubs and trees (among other accolades) admired dogwoods. On his birthday on February 22, 1785, he recorded in his diary that he had removed from the woods a "Mount Vernon" shrubbery to plant and then on March 1st he wrote of the planting of "a circle of Dogwoods with a red bud tree in the Middle, close to the old cherry near the South Garden House."

The wood of the dogwood has extremely high resistance to sudden shocks, similar to hickory wood. Because the wood can be hammered without splitting or mushrooming out, it has been a favorite for the heads of golf clubs and for the handles of chisels. It has been used for mauls, mallet heads, wedges, knitting needles, spindles, yokes, hay forks, barrel hops, machinery bearings, and rake teeth. Jewelers prefer dogwood sticks for cleaning lenses since they do not scratch the glass. In the last century, 90 percent of the dogwood trees cut were used to make shuttles for the textile industry. Dogwood shuttles would not crack under the continuous strain of carrying the weft thread or from being in continual contact with the threads of the warp. It would wear smoother, not rougher, with use.

An interesting tidbit is this historical usage of the dogwood's bark, now obsolete. The native Americans used the aromatic bark, especially the inner bark of the root, to treat malaria! A naturally occurring alkaloid cornin or cornic (gallic) acid, gives the bark astringent properties. Because of the bark's bitter taste, apparently the pioneers would go a step further and steep it in whiskey to imbibe whenever! Native Americans also used the root bark to produce a scarlet dye for blankets, feathers, and belts.

When Mark and Patty were living in Santa Fe, New Mexico (1992-1994), Sally and I visited several pueblos and the Bandelier National Park. (Mark completed his post-doctoral studies at Los Alamos National Lab after defending his Ph.D. dissertation in 1992 at Boston University.) We bought a Navajo wall hanging to remember our visit. The wool rug has beautiful colors, both natural and naturally dyed, and a spirit cut.

As referenced before, Julia Ellen Rogers in *The Tree Book*, (1916, vol. 9), waxes poetic about the grace and beauty of the dogwood's leaves, with their channeled curving and clustered fruit: "Most people miss the loveliness of graceful line and delicate colour harmony revealed by leafless trees. I am happy to say it is a curable form of blindness."

Red Osier or Red Dogwood

Red dogwood grows wild on our beach and in the woods atop the stream bed that angles across our property from Griggs Creek. It is a medium-sized deciduous shrub, about four to five feet tall. Its underground stolons allow it to spread in the shade, forming dense thickets of branches and twigs that have various dark red colorations. The small dull white flowers appear in clusters that are about one to two inches wide. Its berries are globose and white. The Latin specific epithet *sericea* means "silky," referring to the texture of the leaves. It is native to North America. Its root system provides excellent soil retention and therefore, the tree is frequently used for waterway bank erosion protection and restoration. It is an attractive shrub even in winter.

The bark of the red osier can be used to made dye. The Lakota, Algonquian, and Ojibwe would take the tree's inner bark and mix it with other plants and minerals to make red dye. They also used the inner bark in smoking mixtures, known as *kinnikinnick*. Native Americans valued the medicinal value of the berries, eating them to treat colds and to slow bleeding. I have also seen marvelous Native American baskets crafted with the tree branches.

From 2010 to 2014, Sally and I served on a Sanilac County water conservation committee, staffed by professors from both University of Michigan and Michigan State. The county received a $400,000 grant to develop and implement a plan to reduce *the amount of fertilizers and pesticides/herbicides entering the water-courses and streams from farms and eventually draining into Lake Huron. We visited numerous farmers to discuss the project and to offer cattle exclusions, or bridges, that could be put over their streams. We also offered to plant riparian shrubs, including red dogwoods, along all the rivulets and streams. As I recall, we persuaded about four or five farmers, out of the dozen or so we interviewed, to participate.*

A master gardener referred me to the poet, Hyam Plutzik (19111962), a Pulitzer Prize finalist and author of several books of poetry. Plutzik wrote this poem called "Because the Red Osier Dogwood." It begins: "Because the red osier dogwood is the winter lightning…" and ends with "… End the cabbage butterfly, and all the families whom the sun fathers in the cauldron of his mercy." It is very profound and interesting.[5]

When I served as pastor at First Lutheran Church of the Reformation in New Britain, Connecticut, the congregation established a large memorial garden in the shape of a Celtic cross. In each quadrant of the cross, we planted a Cornus sousa, a Japanese flowering dogwood tree. The trees were purchased and cared for by Mrs. Evelyn Anderson. The shrubs flourished, bearing wonderful red strawberry-sized berries, thanks to Evelyn's gardening skills.

---

[5] "The Red Osier Dogwood" by Hyam Plutzik

BETULA papyrifera, aka paper birch or white birch

Paper Birch or White Birch

Have you ever used birch branches for punishing errant children? I hope not! Although it is interesting that the generic name, *Betula* derives from the Latin word for "beat." Ugh! White birch, canoe birch or paper birch, is so named because of its thin, chalky-white bark that often peels in paper-like layers from the trunk.

The birch is a relatively short-lived species, living about seventy-five to one hundred and twenty-five years. It is native to the northern part of North America. There are some thirty-five species around the globe, without much variance. The white birch self-seeds very easily and is often one of the first species to colonize a burned area. The birch growing throughout our property, both on the beach and in the woods, is self-seeded.

The tallest birch tree in the United States is in Cheboygan County, Michigan. Its clump of trunks arise over ninety-three feet from a base about six feet thick. Paper birch is the state tree of New Hampshire and the arboreal emblem of Saskatchewan, Canada.

Birches are good biochemists. Their leaves are rich in resins and their bark is rich in both phenolics and carbolic acid. Birch resins are aromatic and have properties similar to synthetic polymers. The bark also contains "betulin" which makes it waterproof, a quality which made the trees invaluable to Native Americans. They used the bark for many purposes, such as snowshoes, baskets, wigwams, and canoes.

Have you ever canoed in a canoe made from birch bark? Victor Silk, the forest ranger we met in the Hiawatha National Forest back in the 1960s, loaned us his birch bark canoe for an afternoon. It weighed only about fifty pounds, light enough to carry into the Coattail Lake, but strong enough to carry twenty times as much weight. At the first stroke of the paddle, we glided over the still lake like a bird, almost silent. I remember savoring the sweet fragrance of the birch. Although other materials were also used to make canoes, many Native Americans preferred birch bark canoes, because they were the lightest, strongest, and most flexible—necessary qualities when shooting sharp rockfanged rapids.

To make a canoe, the bark is stripped from the wood in strips and sewn together with the slender roots of tamarack trees as thread. These bark strips are then stretched and tied over a frame, typically made of northern white cedar. All holes in the bark and cracks in the seams are calked over with the resin of northern pine or balsam fir.

Betula papyrifera is important as a staple winter food for deer and moose, which browse on the bark. Unfortunately, it is of poor nutritional value because it contains large quantities of lignin, making digestion difficult. However, the inner bark of birch, rich in oil and starch, has been used for centuries as food by humans in times of famine.

Guy Sternberg, author of a great reference book, *Native Trees for North American Landscapes* (2014), raises up the wellbeing of the paper birch as an alarm of global warming: "According to predictions, this phenomenon will increase the occurrence of heat waves and drought caused by human-induced escalations in atmospheric concentrations of the greenhouse gases that trap radiant heat. The loss of beautiful trees, like paper birch, will be one of the early warning signs that human species has irrevocably fouled it nest." Where is Greta Thunberg when we need her?

Once when Sally and I were birding with Dr. Napier Shelton, ornithologist and author, amidst the bogs and streams of Sanilac County, we came upon a beaver dam constructed of birch branches in the blueberry bogs off of Interstate 46. Amazingly waterproof! On the same outing, we identified almost fifty species of birds and scared up a group of feeding whooping cranes, almost as large as a herd of deer. It was a remarkable one-day adventure.

MALUS
The Apple Tree

An aged "eating" apple tree was on the north side of the driveway when we purchased the property in 1977. The tree still bore small apples. Sally would gather some to peel and bake into apple pies. Even her mother, Cristeta Lorenzana (Alvarez) Santos, while she lived with us for several years, helped peel the apples. Even though the apples were small—and suffered from apple scab, apple rust and fireblight (we have never used herbicides)—they just diced and remove the diseased sections. Over the years, I have planted six to eight different apple trees, several of which have borne fruit. The most productive have been the two heritage apple trees planted on the lakeside plot.

Apple trees can display fruit with a wide range of color and size. Some of my favorite varieties are Cortland, Liberty and Gala. Worldwide, there are over 1,000 cultivars of apple trees in existence.

Each spring, my wild "sweet" crabapple trees, standing on the edge of our property, bursts into colorful bloom on naked wood. Once its fruit develops and ripens, every youngster that sees the crabapple pomes are ready to set their teeth in them. But invariably, the intense acidity discourages a second bite! Fresh crabapples are palatable only to animals and birds, especially Grosbeaks, who love them.

Apparently, when the French botanist and explorer, Francois Michaux, tasted a crabapple he exclaimed: "--pity Americans for never tasted fine Normandy wine, cider or jams." Indeed, the early settlers did make fine jelly, jams, cider and wines from American crabapples, and these delicacies grace our tables still today.

My major reference book is *The Manual of Cultivated Trees and Shrubs Hardy in North America* (1960, 2nd ed.), by Alfred Rehder (18631949), the foremost taxonomist, dendrologist, and botanist at the Harvard Arnold Arboretum from 1898 to1940. Rehder was naturalized in 1904 and received an honorary master's degree in 1913. He identified and named over sixty plants. For example, he identified and named three related species of crabapples, describing them as having similar leaf blades but narrower (*Malus lancifolia*) or with truncate-shortened (*Malus glaucescens*) or heart-shaped (*Malus glabrata*), and each having fruits either markedly flat on the sides, or nearly spherical, or distinctly broader than high (*Malus platycarpa*). Whew! He eventually grouped these three species together as one variable species, realizing that by sensible gradations the most extreme forms merge into each other.

Can you imagine the story of William Tell with the apple left out? There are abundant instances of apples featured in folklore and literature, too numerous to enumerate here, but here is one of my favorites. The biblical book, Song of Songs, also known as the Song of Solomon or simply "Canticles," is unique in that, unlike the other books of the bible, it exhibits no interest in law or covenant or even God. Instead, it celebrates sexual love, giving voice to two lovers, praising each other, proffering invitations to enjoy. With teasing comments, the pair compete in flattering compliments of allegory: "…my beloved is to me as a cluster of henna blossoms in the vineyards of En Gedi, an apple tree among the trees of the wood, a lily among brambles," as they share their bed under the forest canopy. Great imagery and symbols of exquisite joy attained through the senses—can you smell the fresh Gala apples?

No chapter about apple trees would be complete without mentioning Johnny Appleseed, *nee* John Chapman (1774-1845). Although born in Massachusetts, he practiced his craft as "nurseryman" in the area of Wilkes-Barre, Pennsylvania. Popular images of him spreading apple seeds randomly everywhere he went are false. In fact, he planted nurseries, rather than orchards, and surrounded them with fencing to protect them from livestock. Once planted, he left the nurseries in the care of neighbors, who sold the apple trees on shares. He returned every several years to tend the nurseries.

His first nursery was planted on the bank of the Brokenstraw Creek, near Warren, Pennsylvania. He went on to establish nurseries in Massachusetts, New York, West Virginia, Ohio, and Indiana. He was a missionary for "The New Church" (Swedenborgian) and inspired many museums and historical sites, most notably the Johnny Appleseed Museum in Urbana, Ohio and the Johnny Appleseed Heritage Center, in Ashland, Ohio. In Fort Wayne, Indiana, where he spent his final years, the minor league baseball team is named the Fort Wayne Tin Caps in his honor.

One final note, Johnny Appleseed was known to the Native Americans for his eccentricity and strange garb. He was admired as one who had been touched by the Great Spirit. Even "hostile" Native American tribes respected him and left him strictly alone. When he died, he bequeathed to his sister over 1,200 acres of valuable nurseries filled with tens of thousands of trees.

CRATAEGUS MONOGYNA
The Common Hawthorn

The name *Crataegus* comes from the Greek *kratos,* meaning "strength" and *akis,* meaning "sharp"—as most thorns are. This small thorny, deciduous tree, standing only twelve to twenty feet tall, is native to North America. It blooms white flowers in summer and bears long lasting red and orange fruits. Its autumn color is variable, ranging from orangish or copper to scarlet—most spectacular. Its common names include quick thorn, thorn apple, May-tree, and whitethorn. Hawthorn has self-seeded throughout our property, but with over one thousand species, I cannot determine with any confidence which species they are—ugh! Does anyone have a clue? I wonder, are the hawthorn's different species even distinguishable to botanists?

The hawthorn's bark is a smooth grey with the older trees developing shallow longitudinal ridged fissures. Its branches sport sharp one-inch long thorns, ouch! The leaves grow spirally arranged on long shoots, which in turn grow in clusters on the spur shoots of the branches. The fruit or pome is sometimes known as a "haw," containing one to five pyrenes resembling the stones of plums and peaches. The hawthorn provides both food and shelter for many birds and mammals. Not just the fruits, but the leaves are also edible in the spring, when they are young and tender. Its flowers are important sources of nectar for butterflies and moths.

When we were in British Columbia, I learned that the indigenous tribe, Kutenai, uses the berries to make black jelly and for medicinal purposes. I believe some Asian cultures use the berries of different

Hawthorn species to produce jams, jellies, juices, alcoholic beverages, and other flavored drinks. However, after researching the side effects of eating the berries, and reading that an overdose can cause arrhythmia, low blood pressure, and even nausea and dizziness, I have not tasted or harvested the berries. I prefer to leave them "for the birds."

PRUNUS SEROTINA
Sour Black Cherry

Prunus, a very large genus, includes most all the trees having stone fruits, like almond, apricot, cherry, nectarine, peach, and plum. Most trees in the genus have alternate leaves, meaning the leaves grown on the stem in a staggered pattern, appearing as if each leaf grows in between the leaves on the opposite side. This means that each plant node only has one leaf growing from it. They are deciduous. The flowers can be pink, white, red, and greenish and are borne in clusters.

Cherry trees are also Prunus and include the ornamental cherry (*serrulata*), choke cherry (*virginiana*), blackthorn, and cherry laurel. Depending on the species, cherry fruit is sour, tart or sweet. Michigan's sour cherry, *serotina*, is one of the few fruit trees to thrive in shady areas. Several grow on our property, having been seeded by birds. Birds will eat the fruits whole and then pass or regurgitate the pits which will germinate wherever soil disturbances (openings in the dirt) are. The seedlings are often able to establish under the forest canopy, before they have sufficient sun light.

The tallest tree of all cherries is the wild cherry. It can grow to about seventy-five feet tall, compared to the ornamental sour cherry which will grow only to about twenty to twenty-five feet tall. The largest on record grows in Great Smokey Mountains National Park, measuring 134 feet in height and nearly six feet in diameter.

Settlers and Appalachian pioneers invented a drink called Cherry Bounce; juice pressed from the fruits and infused in a brandy or rum cordial which, though bitter, was a favorite of old-timers. As long ago as

1820, travelers in Kentucky, Ohio, and Michigan sent barges tethered to large flat boats down the Ohio River to New Orleans, loaded with flour, bacon, whiskey, tobacco, horses, cherry wood and, of course, Cherry Bounce for the French Orleans market.

The wood of the cherry tree is most precious and is used for cabinets and furniture (both solid and veneer), as well as for various tools and implements. Durable, strong, and close-grained, it will last forever.

> *When I was a boy in the 1940s, I took a streetcar to downtown Cleveland with Mrs. Dorothy Jarus, a neighbor, to trade and collect stamps. I recall the paneling of the Pullman wooden streetcars—superb cherry! I find it astonishing to remember. Today, boards of such dimensions are not readily available, and are prohibitively expensive.*

Cherry wood takes a handsome finish, shrinks but little, and warps not at all if seasoned, no matter the temperature or moisture changes in the air. I have seen stains and varnishes used on cherry wood to give it a "mahogany" look. Indeed, mahogany and cherry can be difficult to tell apart when finished off with stain, but why would anyone want to alter cherry?

Wild cherry belongs to one of the most disease and insect prone tree families, but *Prunus serotina,* our tree (the Michigan sour cherry), is the most troubled tree of them all.

Its twigs and leaves contain high levels of hydrocyanic or prussic acid, making them toxic to livestock and humans. Cherry bark, on the other hand, has been used in the manufacture of prussic acid cough medicines. Native Americans boiled and brewed the inner bark and roots to make sedative tea and astringent wash. The secretions have a bitter almond taste. Or so I surmise. You can smell the bark and its secretions, but do not lick or taste the broken limbs or leaves!

Although we would be poisoned by the foliage, a host of insects, mites and over two hundred species of butterfly and moth caterpillars find shelter in the cherry and devour its leaves—often defoliating entire trees! Have you ever seen a most conspicuous black warty, parasitic knot fungus growth on the cherry's twigs and small branches? I often wondered what these tumor infested appearances were, noticing that the trees could carry the warty growths for years. They are actually the tree's response to irritation by insects or fungi. In defense, the tree has small double glands on the leafstalks which secrete sweet nectar, which in turn attract beneficial insects in the hope they will dine on the invaders.

Since there are thirty species of *Prunus* native to North America, let me mention only three, each of which is an ornamental tree, all quite beautiful.

Prunus pennsylvania is a relatively fast growing tree, but not very long lived. It is hardy enough to survive in the Great Lake states. In the fall, it has a brilliant fiery orange color. We have enjoyed seeing them on the shores of Lake Superior near our Upper Peninsula property.

Prunus virginiana is a "suckering" shrub, sprouting suckers from its roots at a considerable distance from its trunk. It can be found in just about all of the Canadian provinces as an understory species, remarkably shade tolerant for a cherry. Familiarly it is called a chokecherry. It has remarkable resilience under variable growing conditions. Its cultivar, called "Canada Red" or "Shubert," has purple leaves. Stunning.

Prunus Caroliniana is an erect evergreen, growing predominantly in the Southeast States, and has inedible shiny black fruits. It is popular in the Deep South. There are specimens in Florida and Texas reaching the height of forty-five to forty-eight feet tall and over three feet in diameter.

"Spring is the season of the eye." I would be remiss if I did not mention the flowering cherries celebrated every year in Washington

D.C. These cherry trees were given to the United States on March 27, 1912 by Mayor Yukio Ozaki of Tokyo, as a sign of friendship. They included twelve different species, although 70 percent are Yashino cherry trees. Japanese cherry horticulture dates back over a thousand years, and focuses on both the size and shape of tree as well as the color, scent, and durability of the flower. The Japanese have also developed notions about where and which species of cherries ought to be planted. Millions of tourists tote their cameras to the annual Cherry Festival, well worth the effort.

Callery or Cleveland Pear

What makes a pear different than an apple, you ask? Flavor is the most important distinguishing factor when eating either fruit, of course. Pears tend to have a fleshy stalk, not joining the fruit in a dip as an apple, but on a bump. They are more granular in texture than apples, gritty when unripe and, when ripe, soon become rotten.

> *I recall eating a pear as a youngster with my paternal grandfather, Bela Moldwin nee Moldovanyi, my Dad's stepfather. (My dad's biological father, Anthony Lovaszi or Lovasy, died in 1908, and my dad was adopted by his stepfather.) Suddenly Grandpa yells out, "I've been stung!" A yellow-jacket had burrowed into his pear and stung the inside of his lip! Beware when eating fruit fresh from the tree.*

Pear trees are twiggy, often thorny, and black in winter, making early spring coverings of delicate white blossoms all the more dramatic and attractive. Botanists trace the history of the pear tree back to Assyria and there is evidence that pear trees were cultivated by Julias Caesar! Species, of which there are about seventy six, grow on every continent except Antarctica. Many produce fruit. Nurseries have hybridized the pear into exotic varieties for different uses, including for use as "street-trees" because of their rapid growth and pollen control. Street-tree pear have all the amenities. The blossoms attract bees, wasps, and butterflies and they exhibit good fall colors of brandy red, golden yellow, and tan. But they do not produce edible large fruit. The fruits of these pears are quite small, just one quarter to one half inch across, and they remain tart until they ripen, when they are quickly eaten by birds.

After 9/11, I read about the only tree which survived the conflagration despite snapped roots and broken branches, a Callery pear. In 2013, the Bartlett Tree Experts and John Brown High School in Queens, New York, began giving seedlings from the surviving, now historic tree, to those organizations which endured tragedy, notably Parkland High School, Parkland, Florida. In 2002, I planted a sapling in the thicket on the west side of our property. It has thrived! Incredibly, it is quite resistant to fire blight.

When I sit on my bench, near the Callery Pear, I reflect and recall the tragic events memorialized by this special tree. Incidentally, the variety I have planted is now marketed as a "Cleveland" Pear, the city of my birth.

Introduced in the United States in 1908, the "Bradford" variety was named in 1963 after Frederick C. Bradford, former director of the USDA Plant Station, Glenn Dale, Maryland.

Pear wood is finally textured and is prized for making woodwind instruments, veneer and woodcuts for artisans.

The father of our friend Joyce Brown, Leonard Gustafson, made curio cabinets from pear wood as Christmas gifts. One graces our home and another John and Jennifer Gustafson's home! Are they related? Our pear cabinet houses my mother's thimble collection.

Mountain Ash or Rowan Tree

The deciduous mountain ash stands tall in my mind's eye, about twenty feet tall, clustered with white flowers and bright orange berries (pomes a quarter of an inch in diameter) and bright postcard-perfect, shiny red foliage in the fall. As the name suggests, it enjoys high elevations and northern latitudes, and prospers in zones two and three. *Sorbus* has about thirty species. The largest *Sorbus americana* specimen is in West Virginia at sixty two feet tall and two feet in diameter. Its bark is smooth and grayish brown, and aromatic when bruised or damaged. Our tree is north of the old apple tree in a thicket and is doing well.

The American mountain ash is also called the "rowan tree," for which the Roan Mountain in North Carolina was named. Its fruits are often called the "holly of the woods" because of its fruits. Roan is derived from a Scandinavian word meaning "red," indicating the color of the fruits. It is related to the European mountain ash.

In the State of Tennessee, the roan tree is called "Peruve," strangely referencing, by analogy, Peruvian bark or Cinchona. The bark of several species of the genus contains quinine, used to treat malaria. Most bitter and aromatic bark was once considered to be antimalarial, imaginary or real, although quinine was an effective treatment for the disease used by the pioneers. Think about homeopathic doctors in Appalachia, then and now.

Strange legends and superstitions, centuries old, cluster around rowan trees and are preserved in the literature of many languages. Its berries, leafy sprays and even chips of its wood were once considered effectual charms to exorcise evil spirits. Rowan trees were planted at the gates of churchyards and by cottage doors. Crosses of "roan" wood, given out on festival days, were worn as amulets, and were tacked over doors of houses and barns.

Although the tree's pomes are not prime wildlife foods, their winter availability can attract grouse, yellow-bellied flycatchers, cedar waxwings, thrushes, and grosbeaks. Old timers in the area, like our neighbor Ed Buresh, have seen the fermented fruit give feeding birds a "buzz." Native Americans, according to John Eastman, in his book, *Forest and Thicket* (1992), used the berries, rich in ascorbic acid, as a tea for preventing or curing scurvy and as a rectal wash for hemorrhoids.

More rowans are coming into cultivation from Europe and Asia, especially China. The hybrids from China stand out for their unique combination of having leaves that turn red, orange and even imperial purple in the fall, and a brilliant red fruit among deep green leaves in the summer.

In September 1960, we moved into the parsonage of Hope Evangelical Lutheran Church at 14300 Bramell Street, Detroit. The church was located at the corner of 9500 Stoepel Avenue and West Chicago Street. The parsonage was a modest three-bedroom brick bungalow, quite comfortable for newlyweds! There was only one tree in the backyard, a mountain ash. At that time, we had only a bed and a table, but no other furniture, no refrigerator or television. We would store the milk and butter in the milk chute to keep it cool. Our dining room table had been shipped to us from the Philippines as a wedding gift from Sally's mother, Cristeta, and her second husband, Jesus Alvarez. (Her first husband, Wenceslao Abriol Santos, died at the age of forty seven in 1951.)

Common Hackberry

The common hackberry, found growing in the Plain States and the moist Great Lake States, develops into a medium to large tree. It has warm yellow leaves and dark purple berry-like fruits with thick skins and a sweet, orange-colored flesh containing a pale brown seed, drooping off of short stalks. In Britain it is called a "bird cherry tree" because birds devour the fruits when they become ripe. Sally and I witnessed a greedy flock of northward-migrating Cedar Waxwings devouring the berries on a hackberry during an Audubon birding tour we took several years ago, a vivid world premiere in color.

The berries are not recommended for human consumption. The Scottish refer to the tree as the "hagberry" tree. Why? I am not sure, but other names include sugar-berry, nettle-tree, and hoop-ash. In October 2019, Todd Paterson, a nurseryman, when removing our fallen 102 year-old poplars, accidentally cut down my beautiful hackberry! I planted a replacement seedling in spring 2020, in the thicket near M-25.

Hackberry is utilized in large, landscaped parks, streets, and open spaces. It grows well under city conditions whether dry, wet or windy. Its wood is used primarily for furniture, fence posts, kitchen cabinets, and the inevitable boxes and crates. Because the wood is tough and flexible, it is still used today for barrel hoops, as in pioneer days.

Hugh Johnson's *The World of Trees*, references Tennyson's poem, "The Lotus-eaters," which portrays mild-eyed, melancholy men witnessing the pollination of the hackberry tree as they were commanded to drink of the fruits to have "courage." They gained courage almost immediately and were enchanted with unworldly beauty, valleys, snowy mountain tops, and mountain clefts covered in streams. Now, I know what really happened. The men ate the lotus-berries, thereby falling under the tree's spell. Too much hackberry wine! They believed they no longer wanted to continue homeward to the "Fatherland," but would rather stay where they were.

Older wild hackberries frequently develop cavities at the site of decaying branch stubs, providing nesting and hibernation sites for many wildlife species. The tree's narrow crotches and numerous spur branches also support many bird nests. Hackberry foliage serves as a primary larval food source for several butterflies, especially the friendly hackberry butterfly which will land on your shoulder to say "hello!'

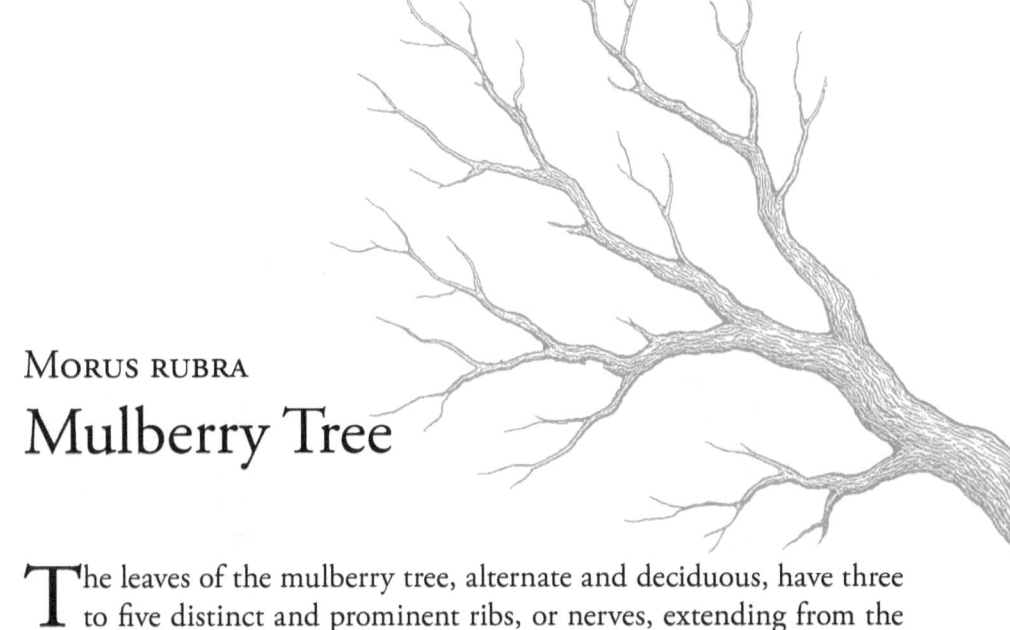

Morus rubra
Mulberry Tree

The leaves of the mulberry tree, alternate and deciduous, have three to five distinct and prominent ribs, or nerves, extending from the base, and may be un-lobed or unequally double lobed, mitten shaped or tri-lobed at the apex. The tree's flowers appear from the axils of the deciduous bud scales of the lower leaves. The fruit is a mass of thinskinned fruitlets with juicy, thick flesh—of a purple color so dark as to be nearly black—surrounding the tiny nutlets. Few fruits stain your hands and clothes as effectively as the red and black mulberry. The mulberry has a way of looking many times its real age, with burs and lichen, inspiring stories and the great affection of mulberry lovers.

The male mulberry trees have catkins that whither and drop after they release their pollen. Their forms, when they are on the ground, are uninteresting. In the air, however, you can see how well designed they are. They rock back and forth, set in motion by wind, dispersing their pollen the way a thurible being waived by a Roman Catholic priest disperses incense. How many are allergic to the pollen and the incense?

We "have" two mulberry trees, one female just over the north boundary into our neighbor's lot and one fruitless male just over the south boundary into our other neighbor's lot. I don't need to plant one! These two trees have grown quickly over the years, and each stands about forty to fifty feet tall. In years past, we have harvested the berries from the north tree by laying down a tarp and climbing the tree to shake the bountiful branches to get enough mulberries for a pie. The fruit is used for jams also, but most often it is a treat for the birds.

A former United States champion tree was at Tower Hill in Illinois, with a trunk nearly seven feet in diameter, and was removed in 2002 by community officials who placed greater value upon sidewalks than preserving a champion tree! The current champion is in Tennessee, reaching over fifty-three feet in height with an equal spread and a trunk eight feet thick. In South Appalachia, red mulberry trees can grow to seventy feet with a trunk almost four feet in diameter.

Commercially, mulberry wood is soft, but rather tough and durable, and used principally for furniture, fence posts, cooperage and shipbuilding.

The hemp plant, important for its fibrous inner bark, and the hop plant, are both well-known herbaceous members of the mulberry family. Hops are used in the brewing of beer and is a staple field crop.

The red mulberry tree is not to be confused with the *Morus alba*, the white mulberry, which produced the "secret of silk" in China for at least 5,000 years. The Chinese domesticated the silkworm moths, which cannot fly, and raised them on white mulberry trees. The caterpillar of the silk moth spins a very fine thread into a cocoon. Mulberry trees were planted in England in the 17th century in the hope of starting a silk industry.

The mulberry tree is referenced in the chronicles of Spanish explorer and conquistador, Hernando de Soto, written in 1540 by a "Gentleman of Elvas," which speak of "mulberry trees, apt to feed silkworms, to make silk …". But, alas, they could make only hemp and ropes from the tree's bark for their brigantines. (de Soto played a role in discovering the province of Florida as well as assisting Pizarro in his conquest of the Inca Empire, Peru.)

In the book, *The Trees of America* (1846), American tree expert Daniel Jay Browne reported that red mulberry had been cultivated in Europe for over a century for its fruit and potentially for silkworm food. He referenced John Clarke, superintendent of the Morodendron Silk Company of Philadelphia, who purported that red mulberry from Missouri yielded a "silk stronger and finer to that of France." Unfortunately for Clarke, silkworms prefer the smoother leaves of the white mulberry. He went out of business!

The predominant problem, if you can call it a problem, is not with the mulberries themselves, but with the birds. After eating the fruit from female trees, they create a purple-black "mess" wherever they roost, usually above a patio or your car.

Sorrel Tree or Sourwood

Sourwood is a strange name for a delightful little tree. One of the most beautiful deciduous trees native to North America, sourwood grows in the wild as an understory tree in the Eastern and Southern United States. Why is it called "sourwood"? Because the leaves are acrid. If you taste them, and yes, I have tasted and chewed the leaves, they are decidedly sour and bitter.

Most notable about the sourwood is the fragrance of its flowers. The flowers' perfume sweetens the summer air and, more importantly, attracts bees. Many claim that sourwood honey is the best honey, with its caramel or butter flavor and a rich aroma. In the opinion of many epicures, it surpasses even the most tangy sage honey of California.

Sourwood honey is considered a delicacy in Appalachia and quite expensive. If traveling there, look for signs along the roadside beside a row of "bee gums" or hives, advertising honey for sale. But if you are buying, you will want to make sure it is sourwood honey, and not honey from mountain laurel or rhododendron bushes. If you do ever see the "bee gums" and road signs, stop and buy me a jar!

The sourwood has an irregular branching habit, giving it a somewhat triangular canopy of slick, leathery foliage. In midsummer, when few other trees are in bloom, the sourwood's long curving raceme of white flowers extends from its branches, looking like a lacy gown or little lilies-of-the-valley outlining the tree's green lustrous leaves. In early fall, these same racemes bear fruiting capsules, which stand upright rather than hanging, and the tree's leaves turn into a dazzling display of reds, scarlets and purples. The capsules, or fruits, split open at maturity when dry, and release the seeds.

The sourwood is one of a kind. In my opinion, it bears a sort of Asian grace because of the way its shoots fall away hearkening the multiple eaves of a pagoda, forming a tall pyramid as high as fifty to seventy feet. The largest sourwood, growing along the Roanoke River, Virginia, is ninety feet tall with a trunk more than three feet in diameter.

Although the sourwood is endemic to North America, it can be found growing wild only in the Eastern United States. It needs hot summers to thrive, and is not easy to grow, making it rather a rarity as an ornamental tree. However, because it is slow growing, it is a good specimen for bonsai. Its roots grow year-round, needing only nutrients and water, because its root hairs feed and concentrate at the outer-most limit of the root system, near the topsoil layers. The deeper roots anchor and hold the plant upright against wind and gravity, and convey water and essential nutrients, nitrogen, phosphorus, and potassium, in solution. Boron, calcium, copper, iron, magnesium, manganese, molybdenum, sulfur and zinc are the minor elements needed. Of course, air and water provide about half of the essential elements for all plants and trees. The sourwood's roots, however, store reserve food carrying the plant through winter. I planted a sourwood in the west thicket, near M-25, on the south side of our driveway. A real beauty, gorgeous in color and shape! So far so good, but we will see if it survives.

The tree's wood is hard, medium-heavy, and has a red-tinged brown heartwood and a very thick layer of paler sapwood. Before plastics, it was used to make wagon sled runners in mountainous regions. Today, it is still used to make tool handles. I am told that hikers in the Appalachians will seek the twigs and leaves for a chew or a brew, depending on how thirsty they are. Once upon a time in the days of home medicine, the leaves were boiled as a tonic with an acidic but not altogether unpleasant taste.

Sourwood belongs to the Ericaceae or heath family and is related to the *Arbutus unedo,* aka the strawberry tree which grows in California, the Mediterranean and Southwest Ireland. The strawberry tree is similarly an understated tree with hundreds of clusters of tiny near-white pitchers blossoming throughout its handsome bay-like leaves.

The strawberry tree's fruits have rough pimply skins but look more like cherries than strawberries. Most people, upon seeing them, will taste one…and only one. It is a dry and disappointing mouthful. In fact, the tree's nomenclature *unedo* means: "I eat one.'

The *Arbutus menziesii*, or the madrone tree, grows in California. Its flowers are more conspicuous than sourwood because they form at branch tips. The madrone tree also grows taller than the sourwood, reaching about eighty to ninety feet at maturity. The madrone's beauty lies in its combination of rich green foliage and beautiful smooth red bark. Its trunk is graceful, curving and forking into limbs.

I have a hand-made locked jewelry box on the fireplace mantle. It was carved from a madrone burr by Native American artist J. Volleen. Nancy St. Clair of Carsonville, Michigan, a friend from the Sanilac Historical Museum, gave the box to us. It is beautifully carved and serves as a memento of our friendship with her; I conducted her funeral at the Sanilac Historical Museum in 2015. The piece's veneer glistens with reddish and brownish hues. Madrone trees are endangered, and it is illegal to cut them down or remove any burrs in most areas.

ULMUS AMERICANA

American Elm

The elm is a magnificent part of urban America and the American rural landscape. It is a living American monument. Its vase-shaped silhouette has cast broad shade over our country's streets and thoroughfares for centuries. It featured prominently in the lives of the earliest settlers and colonists and, as late as the 1970s, about 70 percent of hedgerow trees in the Eastern United States were elms.

The elm's wood is as strong as it is supple and in pioneer times, it was used for the hubs of heavy wagons because it was able to resist all the pressure and friction brought to bear on it. In the first half of the twentieth century, whenever shock-resistance was essential, whether for agricultural implements, building ships, or flooring, elm wood was employed. It was the leading wood in barrel staves, boxes, crates, and household woodenware. Historians tell us that in 1946, over two hundred million board-feet of elm, most of it cut from Ohio and Wisconsin, was utilized in one year alone.

I recall the elms in the back yard of Mrs. Pearl Stavers' Northwest Detroit home and arching over most Detroit streets for decades, until the attack of Dutch elm disease. Dutch Elm Disease—identified in the Netherlands in 1921, is the fungus *Ophiostoma novo-ulmi* or *Ceratocystis ulmi*, and is spread by bark beetles. It reached Ohio in 1930. The fungus spores are carried by the shiny beetles as they bore into the bark and tunnel vertically to lay larvae. Experimental remedies, ranging from insecticide sprays to tree inoculations have had little success. Hopefully the elms will develop their own immunity to deter the fungus.

The DNA in most animals, including humans, is diploid, consisting of two sets of chromosomes. But plants and trees are malleable, many with four or six sets of chromosomes. American elms, botanists tell us, were thought to be all tetraploids, containing four sets of chromosomes. But in the 1990s, scientists tested several elm trees which tolerated the Dutch elm disease and discovered that they had three, not four sets of chromosomes. Did they inherit their disease resistance from the diploid?

We have several American elms on our property. One large, beautiful tree is on the lake side of our home and has been thriving since we bought the house in 1977. Why has it been spared? Chromosomes? Immunity? Location? Lake effect? Or ants? Yes, ants. Every spring I lace twigs and leaves with apple honey and place them around the tree. The honey attracts black carpenter ants which, I hope and pray, eat the beetle larvae. As soon as they say an elm has tolerated the fungus, I'll buy one. Let me dream with Virgil:

> Full in the midst a spreading elm displayed a trembling leaf with some light vision impregnated with airy dreams.

In early spring, goldfinches and purple finches flock to our fruiting elms. All sorts of migratory birds use them for emergency food. Northern (Baltimore) orioles love the drooping boughs as nesting sites. Fearful that I might lose my elms, I planted a related species, the Japanese elm, *Zelkova serrata* (*Ulmaceae* elm family), in the thicket on the west side of the property near M-25. It has a different set of chromosomes than the American elm, which may allow it to resist the fungus. So far so good.

> *On the Yale University campus square, where deepest traditions abound, Sally and I once sang with the New Britain Chorale, in the mid 90s, under a colonnade of elms. It was a beautiful fall for an outdoor concert, singing four-part harmony on four corners, but the concert was a bust! We ended up singing to the trees.*

Zelkova serrata
Japanese Zelkova

The *Zelkova* is an elm-like tree native to Japan, Korea and China. It has a vase-shaped growing habit and multiple short trunks that grow from fifty to eighty feet tall. It has a round top and its arching branches sport medium-sized, dark green, saw-toothed leaves that turn yellow in summer. Besides its uniquely shaped leaves, it has a thin bark that continually flakes off, exfoliating and revealing enticing little patches of unusual orange colors. A real eye-catcher.

The tree's spring buds, even when flowering, are inconspicuous. I can look and look and still miss the tiny buds and flowers. It is monoecious, and quite hardy. With good soil and drainage, a Japanese elm should live about one hundred years. It is known for its resistance to Dutch elm disease, at least for now. Hugh Johnson, best known for his wine books, in *The World of Trees*, published in 2010 (which I bought immediately upon publication and find a valuable resource) predicts that Dutch elm disease will "eventually kill them also." I hope he is proven wrong!

William Robinson (1838-1935), an Irish botanist and gardener, was attracted to this rare tree. He wrote about the *Zelkova* in his book *The English Flower Gardener*: "(its) really rare (leaves), with longer points, sharper teeth, more numerous nerves and leathery texture, together with the fact that they hang longer, may enable anyone to tell the leaf of the Japanese *Zelkova* from that of the better-known Caucasian tree." Upon reading that, I had to ask: "what's a zelkova?" Nevertheless, I quickly planted one in the thicket on the west of the property, near its distant kin, the nettle aka hackberry. After a few years, it is finally thriving, even after rabbits ate its initial tender leaves.

Because the Japanese *Zelkova* is considered disease and pollution resistant, it is often used for street trees as a substitute for elms. In Japan, it is fashioned into furniture, cabinets and "taiko" drums. It is the symbol of many Japanese cities because of its beauty and colors.

Populus deltoides

Poplar Or Eastern Cottonwood

The poplar tree is a large, fast-growing deciduous tree with a broad, open round-shaped habit. It will grow fifty to eighty feet tall. Poplars are native from Eastern North America through the Great Plains, and typically grow along streams and rivers in lowland areas and swamps. Tiny flowers appear separately in catkins on male and female trees. (If the male and female flowers grow on separate trees, it means the tree is deciduous.) I am sure you have seen the abundant densely-tufted seeds with silky white hairs, giving them the appearance of cotton, blowing through the air and collecting along gutters, curbs, porches, and fences. Yes, cottonwoods shed immense amounts of pollen. In early spring the catkins appear on the branches and drop in about three weeks. Not until these flowers fall do the leaves appear, coppery and strikingly handsome. Then in mid-spring, the seed pods burst, loosening the downy seeds in great quantities upon the wind.

There were four great big poplars, each over a hundred years old, growing in our woods. The four were taken down on August 25, 2017, by the tornadic winds caused by hurricane Harvey, a category four hurricane that devastated the Caribbean and Texas. After they fell, we left their shallow roots and stumps in the woods not only because they were too huge and expensive to remove, but for the benefit of the many woodland inhabitants (mainly insects) sustained by the death of these gigantic trees. It took over a week of work using chainsaws to clear the fallen wood. I estimated the trees' ages at about 105, by counting the annual rings or growth cycles on each horizontal cross section cut through the trunks. Imagine, the seeds must have germinated during WWI!

"We do not inherit the Earth from our fathers,
we are borrowing it from our children."
- Davie Brower, the first executive director of Sierra Club.

Brower has lectured around the world hundreds of times on "CPR" for the Earth: Conservation, Preservation and Restoration, and I am proud that he signed my copy of his book, *Let the Mountains Talk, Let the Rivers Run*. Although oft quoted, Brower's words have become a mantra for me as I tend our patch of wilderness. Our two acres are not only a sanctuary for me to meditate and to realize that a wildness exists within all of us, but an opportunity to raise theological and philosophical questions. How can one look at trees but not see their living sustaining significance, nor understanding the science, nor even know about their mycorrhizal fungi. I left the massive cottonwood stump roots unattended *because* the thread-like massive fungus, which was vital for the old trees' roots to absorb nutrients, would develop a new symbiotic relationship with other vascular plants and nearby living trees as well! Amazing!

We still have several poplars growing throughout our property, with a good specimen at the northeast corner of our property line near the beach. The year round breeze off of Lake Huron rustles the poplar's leaves, keeping it almost in perpetual motion, the sound mimicking the waves rushing on the beach.

Mark and Patty have a large cottonwood at the mouth of their driveway, probably "only" about sixty to eighty years old. The life of a cottonwood is generally short, with 100-120 years being exceptional. Yet, in compensation, it grows faster than any other tree, four to five feet a year! A current national champion grows in a pasture near Minidoka dam, Idaho, measuring only eighty-five feet tall, but its trunk is eleven and a half feet or three and a half meters thick!

Although healthy poplars resist disease and infestations, their roots will mischievously lift up sidewalks, clog water and plumbing lines, and unfortunately invite attacks by defoliators such as beetles, borers, aphids, caterpillars and other bothersome insects. They are susceptible to dieback, cankers, leaf spots, rusts, powdery mildew, and scale. And their bark and branches are easily damaged by every force on the Great Lakes: lightning, ice, wind, and decay. They're really "poplar"!

The photographer, Edward Curtis (1868-1952), chronicled the ancient ways of Native Americans, and included in his documentation the importance of trees, especially cottonwoods. I appreciated especially two of his photographic illustrations: a dramatic image of a Navaho weaver's loom set beneath the exposed root of a cottonwood, and a ceremonial hat made from cottonwood leaves for the Sun Dance of the Cheyenne. The Arapaho believed the stars were cast into the sky by great cottonwoods shedding their cotton seeds. Early American settlers and prairie pioneers similarly revered this great tree. They built fences, corncribs, cabins, stables, ox yokes, saddleries, and coffins from cottonwood. Lewis and Clark referenced scores of trees, including cottonwoods, in their journals of the expedition to look for a northwest passage (1803-1806). Three states have designated the cottonwood as their official state tree: Kansas, Nebraska and Wyoming.

Several years ago, as a certified master gardener, I gave a lecture on trees and shared a poem about my dead *Populus alba* (white poplar).

Ode to My Dead Cottonwood

Listening to your arthritic and creaky joints I waited
Listening to your wind washed grayish bark I waited
Listening to muscular blackish fissured bole I waited
Listening to the thick Riverbank wild grapes curling
up your branches I waited
*   Listening to the Turkey vulture roost at the top*
the lightning damaged cap I waited
*   Suddenly...you spoke I listened to the unsettled*
agitated call of the Cathartes aura with a red head I
listened
*   to the scattering brown ground squirrels I listened*
to the scratch claws of the raccoon in its cavity I listened
to the Downy and Harry rapping I listened to the

Titmice snapping up aphids, eggs and mealy bugs I
listened
> *to my dead (?) Cottonwood and I became alive,*
doffed my hat and said: "Thank you Jesus."

My favorite jazz singer, Billie Holiday (1915-1959), recorded this song, originally a poem written by teacher Abel Meeropol in 1939, to protest thousands of lynchings at the turn of the century in the South. The metaphor links a poplar tree's fruit with lynching victims.

Southern trees bear a strange fruit
Blood on the leaves and blood on the root
Black bodies swingin' in the Southern breeze
Strange fruit hangin' from the poplar trees[6]

---

[6] Lyricsfreak.com. 2015. Strange Fruit Lyrics – Billie Holiday. [online] Available at: http://www.lyricsfreak.com/b/billie+holiday/strange+fruit 20017859.html [Accessed 4 November 2021].

POPULUS TREMULOIDES

Quaking Aspen

Among the twenty-nine poplar species, my favorite is the quaking aspen, with its leaves almost constantly quivering in trembling motion. The aspen's long leafstalks appear flattened, in planes at right angles, not round, and are as flexible as ribbons. Even the slightest breeze causes the tree's characteristic flutter. The language of the Onondaga Native Americans has a phrase referring to the tree: *Nut-ki-e*, meaning "noisy leaf." And an old Russian adage described it thus: "A tree that trembles without even a breath of wind."

Julia Rogers cites a lugubrious wight who imagines the aspen accursed by being the tree on which Judas Iscariot hanged himself, and doomed "ever afterward to shudder and tremble on account of its connection with the tragedy of Calvary."

The aspen has gorgeous yellow colors in the fall. With its golden foliage, shivering on white stems and backlit by clumps of associated dark evergreens, it is surely the most popular of all nature subjects for calendar photographs! I planted one in honor of Dr. J. Lawrence and Charlotte Hill in 2020, in the center of the circular driveway.

As other poplars, like the cottonwood and the willow, the aspen grows quickly, about four to twenty-five feet a year with good soil and weather conditions. It is also short lived and ordinarily small, growing only thirty to forty feet in height with a trunk diameter of eight to twenty-five inches. The largest known quaking aspen is in Ontonagon County at the western end of the upper peninsula of Michigan. It is 109 feet tall and more than three feet in diameter. Huge!

Both male and female cones are hanging catkins, emerging before the leaves. Pollination is driven by the wind. Individual ramets on the cones begin flowering only after fifteen to seventeen years, thereafter producing abundant seed crops every fourth or fifth year. The seeds need only bare, high-calcium soil and plenty of moisture to germinate.

Aspens occupy a larger range than any other North American tree, spreading more than 110 degrees longitude through nine time zones and 47 degrees latitude, from Northern Canada to central Mexico. It grows from sea level up to the timberline. The quaking aspen is the arboreal emblem of the Yukon. Utah has designated the quaking aspen it's state tree.

The aspen is not an individual tree, but a "clone" of trees having identical characteristics and sharing a root structure. The clone extends more than a hundred separate stems, called ramets or suckers, from its original roots, and can spread over eighty feet. The clonal root systems can survive indefinitely. Some botanists surmise that it may be among the oldest living organisms on the planet. A clonal aspen in Minnesota has been aged at about 8,000 years old. The individual ramets generally begin to deteriorate after thirty-five or forty-five years but have been documented to live eighty years. Amazing.

An aspen clone in Utah has 47,000 stems and is estimated to have a total mass of at least three times greater than the world's largest individual tree of any other species. It weighs in with a mass of more than 6,000 tons, one of the largest living organisms on the planet. Can you guess how old it is? Thousands of years? Estimates are 80,000 years!

John C. Loudon (1783-1843), Scottish botanist and author (and the first to use the term "arboretum"), believes that fast growing cloning aspens took over the ruins of Moscow in 1813, after Napoleon ransacked and reduced most of the city to ashes. It is true that aspens are often the first trees to appear after a forest fire.

Aspen's major commercial use is to make pulpwood for books and magazines, but it is also used as material for crating, matches, excelsior, and interior trim. Native Americans used aspen for medicinal purposes, making solutions from the bark to treat colds, fevers, coughs, and menstrual pain. The bitter bark does contain salicin, an ingredient in aspirin. In particular, Crees used the sweetish inner bark for food, and the Chippewas tapped the tree for sap.

Hairy woodpeckers, yellow sapsuckers and ruffed grouse nest in both living and decaying aspens. Porcupines and bears enjoy the foliage as a summer choice of food. More than three hundred insects also like to forage on the aspen. Its foremost insect pest is the common tent caterpillar (*Malacosoma disstria*). You may not see them feeding on the leaves, but you will see the silken mats or webs on the aspen's branches and trunks. As a defense mechanism, the aspen will manufacture phenol compounds that act as a natural insecticide. (I have been known to lop off web covered branches to burn them.)

The family of aspens include numerous cultivars and hybrid specimens, including two Chinese poplars, *Populus lasiocarpa* and *Populus simonii*. Both have beautiful unique and emphatic leaves on long stalks, and neither of which do I have. If I only had a bit more acreage...

FRAXINUS AMERICANA
White Ash

There are about forty species of *Fraxinus* or ash including white, green, and blue ash. Each of these three are quite similar. They commonly reach seventy to eighty feet, with a diameter of two to three feet at chest height. Ash has a straight trunk and a round topped crown. Its branches extend quite close to the ground. There is documentation of a three hundred year-old white ash reaching 175 feet tall with trunks about five feet in diameter in the Eastern United States. All trees of that age and size have vanished.

Guy Sternberg, author of a great reference book *Native Trees for North American Landscapes*, ruminates and reflects on the ash tree. It is one of the fastest growing strong-wooded shade trees in North America, known for its outstanding fall color. Born in 1947, Sternberg is owner and operator of Starhill Forest Arboretum, Petersburg, Illinois; former staff (32 years) at the Illinois State Department of Natural Resources; and adjunct professor in Biology at Illinois College. He holds numerous awards, consults around the world, and supports numerous public service projects. He is my favorite "go to" arborist.

The white ash is dioecious and grows singly. Its white flowers are wind pollinated. The male trees bloom annually. The female trees set major crops once every several years, when they bloom heavily. The tree's fruits are winged samaras or "keys" and often remain on the tree, in drooping clusters, throughout the winter. In autumn, the foliage turns a distinct maroon or reddish green. When we had more than twenty ash on our property (now we have only several) neighbors asked if they could forage for black and arrowhead morel mushrooms under the trees! I do recall a couple of years when they found several handfuls to take home.

Early pioneers, Native Americans, and even Norwegians immigrants to the United States were convinced that white ash leaves were highly offensive to snakes, particularly rattlesnakes, and would stuff them in boots and leggings to prevent bites. Also, when swallowed, a concoction of ash buds and bark was said to a be a sure remedy for snakebite. No medical evidence supports these claims. Aphrodisiac effects have similarly been attributed to the seeds.

White ash wood is strong, tough, hard, and pliant, making it ideal for tools and agricultural implements, spades, shovel handles, hammers, etc. (Whole books have been written on the usage of ash!) I have seen ash used for church pews and floors, and even for bowling alleys here in Deckerville, Michigan. Whenever you want strength and lightness, important for oars, paddles, keels, boats, staves, garden and porch furniture, drays, wagons, and even airplanes, call on ash.

I remember the smell of peanuts and Ball Park Franks with mustard at Tiger Stadium and the ringing "tock" of the bat. Once, when we were in the bleacher seats with our three children, we sat through a rain delay of about two hours, enjoying peanuts, popcorn, and cracker jacks. We were overjoyed to finally "feel" the cracking sound of the bat when the game resumed and the batters returned to the plate. Most bats in those days were the Louisville Slugger, made of ash for its strength and springiness. I still have a couple ash bats at home.

The tradition of ash baseball bats changed in the 1990s. It was then that an iridescent green beetle, the emerald ash borer, hopped a ride into the United States on a shipment from Asia. By 2005, *Nature* magazine and the United States Forest Service conservatively estimate, more than fifty million trees were killed the previous decade. It costs more than two billion dollars a year nationwide to remove the trees killed by invasive insects and diseases. Researchers have been breeding hybridized varieties of ash in response, to at least slow down infestations long enough to find ways to stop them altogether. We have lost most all of the ash trees on our property. I have cut down at least twenty "mature" trees, burning them to eliminate the larvae of the beetle, to no avail.

When the ash borer felled several of our ash trees, we removed the trunks and limbs from our thicket, and gave them to our friend, Henry Dyterhuis, a carpenter and farmer living in Ontario. With his special Dutch artistry, he fashioned them into mantles for our double-sided fireplace. If ever you visit our home, please take a look at the special beauty in its grain. Henry also constructed all of the white oak cabinets in the kitchen by begging, borrowing and stealing wood from local farmers. He charged me only two dollars per linear foot! Henry was a marvelous craftsman. We met him at the farmers market in St. Jacob, Ontario. While building our house, 2000-01, Sally, her mother, "Mama" and I made ten trips to the Dyterhuis home to pick up cabinets, chairs and toys. Henry made four trips to our home to install the cabinets.

In addition to the ash borer, white ash is also a favorite host of the fall webworm (*Hyphantria cunea*), a tiger moth caterpillar that builds communal tent-like enclosures tightly around the foliage branch tips. I have seen hornets sting and carry away the caterpillars to their nests near our garage. I am hopeful that white ash will someday develop an immunity against diseases and beetles.

Since our son-in-law, Don Larsen, is of Norwegian descent, and our son, Mark, was a Fulbright scholar in Bergen, Norway, let me conclude this chapter with Norse mythology. *Yggdrasil* was a sacred ash tree who supported the universe and had mystical powers. Its branches "spread over the whole world, and even above heaven." At the top sat an eagle; at the bottom, a dragon; in between, a squirrel, scrambling up and down endlessly relaying threats and counter-threats between the eagle and the dragon.

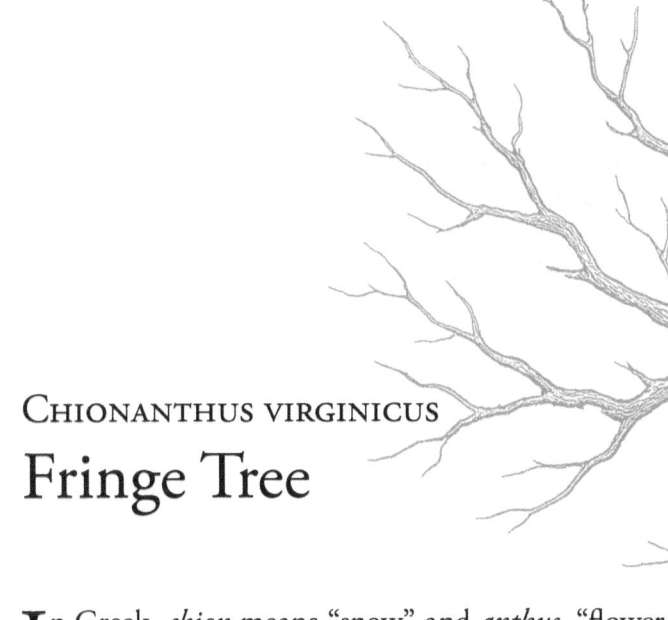

Chionanthus virginicus
Fringe Tree

In Greek, *chion* means "snow" and *anthus*, "flower." The fringe tree is also known as the flowering ash or the Old Man's Beard.

The fringe tree is indigenous to the United States and can be found scattered in moist wooded areas and swamp borders. Despite its preference for warmer climates, it can also be found along the Atlantic Coast and up through Canada in Quebec and Ontario. A fringe tree at Mount Vernon, Virginia, near George Washington's former house in Fairfax County, stands thirty-two feet tall with a trunk seventeen inches across.

My fringe tree, planted in our front courtyard, really should not have been planted at all. The fringe tree really only thrives in the Southeastern States and does not like harsh climates. Yet our tree survives. Although it struggles year after year through our winters, it is stunningly beautiful when its belated leaves unfold and its delicate fringe-like white flowers blossom. The flowers appear like a bridal veil. On the female tree (it is dioecious) the drooping blossoms broaden to reveal blue fruits in late summer. The fruits are unusual and quite ornamental, and enjoyed by many species of birds including turkeys.

Once when I was sitting in our courtyard admiring my fringe tree and the five spidery-thin petals at the base of a leaf, neighbors called over and asked, "What are you looking at?" I lifted up a flower and shared how excited I was because my tree rarely bloomed. After my response, they nodded as if it was nothing special. So often people look, but don't see!

The fringe tree is closely related to ash and olive trees. Although it has no real economic importance, members of our Sylva Garden Club boast about its beauty. I believe it deserves to be introduced into most gardens because of its most ethereal showy flowers. In autumn the leaves turn clear bright yellow. A feast for weary eyes.

Basswood

Basswood was among the first trees cultivated in North America, grown both as a honey plant and for its light carvable wood. There are about twenty-odd species of basswood, not counting Asiatic ones of which little is written. English horticultural author John Loudon cites 1752 as the confirmed introduction date of the tree to the United States, and at least one record indicates that the tree was cultivated in London in 1730.

Early French explorers called the basswood *bois blanc* or "white wood" and gave the same name to two islands in Lake Michigan where the tree was prominent. The tree's English name is a corruption of the term "bast wood," which refers to the tree's fibrous inner bark or bast. Bast was used for cordage and matting. In Berlin, Germany, the famous *Inter den Linden* was named for the rows of European basswood, a smaller species, but beautiful as well.

Basswood can grow for 150 to 200 years, often reaching a height of 130 feet. During a historical reconstruction project at the Lincoln Home National Historic Site, Springfield, Illinois, in 1993, workers discovered several average looking basswoods which were thought to be about fifty years old. After dendrologists examined the trees, they determined that the trees dated back before the Civil War from the late 1850s.

Europeans used basswood to make instruments and fine furniture, including the carved fronts of many pulpits. In both Europe and North America, it was often used for turnery by artisans to craft bowls prior to the advent of lathes. Well, only if the wedding sequence from Henry

Wadsworth Longfellow's "Hiawatha" is to be believed: "Sumptuous was the feasts at Hiawatha's wedding. All the bowls were made of basswood, white and polished very smoothly." Native Americans, specifically the Iroquois, use the wood for carving woodenware, apiary supplies, veneer, wood pulp and excelsior-shavings for packing materials. As noted above, the bark from young shoots is used to make twine, matting, and baskets. Pioneer farmers used twisted sections of the bark as binding for hauling logs.

In the early 1990's, while pastor of First Lutheran Church of the Reformation, New Britain, Connecticut, I presided at a tribal wedding for a Micmac (Mi'Kmag) and his wife. The groom was an artisan wood carver who made carousel horses. As a thank you, I was presented with the carved red mask which is now displayed in our home gallery. I am not sure but I believe the mask is made of basswood.

Basswood has large heart shaped leaves with lopsided bases and cream-yellow, fragrant flowers. Its flower clusters hang from ribbon-like bracts, which do not drop but remain to dangle the nuts into midwinter. Basswood trees begin flowering after about fifteen years, thereafter producing a seed crop almost every year.

The basswood sprouts prolifically from its roots or stumps, forming a circular clump around the tree. Its roots plunge deep and wide and it is rarely upended by strong winds. In the fall, its big leaves turn mottled yellow and drop, adding an assortment of minerals—calcium, magnesium, nitrogen, potassium and phosphorus—to the soil. Unfortunately, basswoods attract small caterpillars, called inchworms or loopers, and other harmful insects such as leaf miners, galls, aphids and moths. Delicately beautiful, pure-white adult moths will migrate far distances to munch on the basswood leaves. The good news is that the common house sparrow serves as a biological control on the moths' larvae. The sparrow was brought to the United States in 1850 specifically for this reason. They are now ubiquitous. You can probably see one if you look outside right now!

I planted a basswood on the south side of our driveway. It attracts hordes of bees and other insects every summer, audible when walking down our drive. Every few years, I remove the sprout clumps surrounding it.

A local farmer claims that no finer honey exists then that produced from basswood flowers. Basswood honey is coveted by gourmets, who regard its slightly minty flavor as exquisite. Euell Gibbons (1911-1975) was an outdoorsman and health food advocate who promoted eating wild foods during the 1960s. I recall the advertisements where he would recommend using pine nuts, catkins, and corms as food supplements by add them to your morning bowl of cereal. He also advertised a hot tea called "tilleul," steeped from dried basswood blossoms. It was marketed as Lipton Linden Tea. Apparently, tilleul is a mild sedative that will calm hysteria, prevent insomnia, and ease cramps. I have never tried it.

Rhus typhina
Staghorn Sumac Tree

The staghorn sumac is easily identifiable any season of the year because of its clubby, dense, velvety twigs that resemble deer antlers. Its twigs, if broken, exude a white latex or milky liquid. In Michigan, the staghorn sumac grows wild along fields and pops up occasionally in the woods. I have heard folks refer disparagingly to sumacs as "ghetto palms" because they grow wild in urban streets and alleys, fencerows and roadsides in major cities. But I think sumacs make beautiful ornamental scrubs despite being commonplace. Henry David Thoreau documents the beauty of sumac in 1854 at Walden Pond: "The sumac grew luxuriantly pleasant leaves, large buds, graceful form, crimson fruit, and how the young sprouts could be bent and broken under the weight of the hordes of bees that were attracted to the plant."

There are about fifty genera and over one hundred species of sumac, or "sumach." Of the six species that I am familiar with that grow in North America, only four of these are identified as trees (and not shrubs). The largest native sumac, the staghorn sumac, is rather small, standing from ten to twenty feet in height. The largest known staghorn sumac tree is growing in Tallapoosa County, Alabama and is currently sixty one feet tall with a trunk fifteen inches thick.

It sprouts from the roots to form thickets, rather than large trunks. The sumac is dioecious and has greenish yellow flowers. Female staghorn sumacs produce sticky, fuzzy, dark red clusters of small berries. The tree has a straggling habit of growth, its forking and often crooked branches form irregular, broad-shaped crowns. The tree's wood is soft and brittle with a satiny appearance and orange to greenish color. Sumac wood is seldom used commercially, but it can be used to make small articles such as napkin rings, picture frames, and darners. The fruits have been used to make an acidic drink derisively called "Indian Lemonade." Most birds seem to regard the fruit as an emergency ration, probably because of its dryness, but ruffed grouse eat the berries frequently, as do deer and squirrels. The bark and roots are rich in tannic acid. Sumacs are subject to attacks by gypsy moths as well as various cankers and vascular wild fungi. John Eastman notes in the book *Forest and Thicket* (1992) that staghorn sumac stems have a thick, soft center that can be poked out easily to make an effective blower for starting a campfire.

As boys, my younger brother, Anthony, and I were taught to recognize poison ivy by means of an old ditty: "Leaflets three, quickly flee." But the jingle does not include poison sumac, which is a treesized relative of poison ivy. Poison sumac resembles poison ivy in both flower and fruit. Its gorgeous coloration, especially during autumn, might tempt one's fingers, but it is best to recall that "good" sumac has finely toothed leaves while the "bad" variety shows only a few low scallops on the leaf margins. Beware! Botanists and scientists agree that the sap of these poisonous trees is the most intense and virulent of all contact poisons in North American. See William Werther's *Some American Trees.*

PLATANUS OCCIDENTALIS &
PLATANUS ORIENTALIS

Planetree or Sycamore

Sycamores are large, deciduous trees that typically have broad irregular silhouettes. They can reach 100 to 150 feet in height and most sources indicate that they will live from 150 to 200 years. However, John Eastman, in his book *Forest and Thicket*, indicates that sycamore trees, if given ideal conditions, can reach an age of five hundred or even six hundred years! I have found no other resource supporting this conclusion, and wonder if he is mistaken. Although in my opinion, Eastman stands out as a reliable resource for the amateur arborist.

The sycamore *orientalis* was planted so widely in mid-seventeenth century London that it gained the name the London plane tree. Most likely it was favored because it is extremely tolerant of urban conditions. The Europeans brought the London plane tree to North America in 1640 to provide shade for travelers and pioneers.

Handel's opera "Serse," which recounts the story of the Persian emperor Xerxes, opens with the emperor singing the aria *Ombra mai fu*: "Ne'er was dappled shade granted so lavishly, so lovingly …." Xerxes was admiring the shade of a plane tree.

It should be noted that in the Middle East, the "sycomore" tree, with a different spelling, does not refer to a plane tree, but to a species of fig trees.

The sycamore's bark is a reddish to gray-brown but, quite unusually, the bark exfoliates in large plates exposing the creamy white and yellowish to orange salmon colored layers beneath. The tree prefers rich soil but will adapt to seasonal flooding, drought and compacted soil conditions. Its abundant fruit balls, which are about an inch in diameter, are retained through the winter.

The leaves vary in size, even on the same branch. The larger leaves develop midsummer and can reach more than ten inches in width and nearly as much in length. The leaves have either three or five shallow lobes and a hollow petiole that encloses the bud. Its spherical reddish flower clusters that appear in the spring, make it a spectacle to behold.

Nancy Ross Hugo waxes elegantly about the visual attractions of the sycamore in the book *Seeing Trees* (a favorite coffee table book of mine):

> Where the stalk, technically a petiole, attaches to the twig, is enlarged, like the cup of a candlesnuffer, it completely surrounded the large, pointed bud beneath (imagine a candlesnuffer surrounding a flame). As soon as the leaf stalk has begun to loosen from the twig you can pull the leaf off and see both the perfect circle inscribed by the leaf scar around the bud and the concave indentation at the end of the petiole where is so perfectly enclosed the bud. This engineering is impressive (…) A second trait is the tree's stipules-leafy outgrowths on either side of the leaf stalk. On most tree species they are inconspicuous, these are quite decorative.

Nonetheless, for me, the tree is special and beautiful not for its adornment of flowers or foliage, but because of its fruitlets, called "buttonwood" balls. The curious fruit is actually hundreds of tightly packed seeds (about eight hundred) that persist on the tree over winter, and then break up into fluff in the spring when the breezes distribute the individual seeds far and wide. I have inadvertently witnessed this amazing sight on several occasions while inspecting my trees.

Sycamore is the most massive of all North American trees. Its trunk exceeds all others in diameter. Large specimens have diameters that range from three to eight feet. In areas of West Virginia, stumps from felled trees have served as dance floors. An exceptionally large one is in Worthington, Indiana, measuring 42.2 feet in circumference. Ancient sycamores in Kashmir, India, boast of girths of sixty feet.

The French explorer and botanist, Andre Michaux (1746-1813), wrote about a sycamore growing on a little island on the Ohio river: "… the circumference of which, five feet from the surface of the earth, forty feet four inches, which makes about thirteen feet in diameter. Twenty years prior to my travels, George Washington had measured this same tree, and found it nearly of the same dimensions." About twenty years later in 1820, Andre Michaux's own son, Francois, found an Ohio sycamore to beat his father's record: "…the trunk of which was swelled to an amazing size; we measured it four feet beyond the surface of the soil, and found it forty-seven feet in circumference. By its external appearance no one could tell that the tree was hollow; however, I assured myself it was by striking it in several places with a billet."

Most sycamores over one hundred years old are hollow at the heart, which does not prevent the tree from continuing to expand through the years. Pioneers often stabled a horse, cow or pig in a hollow sycamore, and sometimes a whole family took shelter in a hospitable giant until a log cabin could be raised.

Sycamore wood is heavy, hard, tough, coarse-grained and difficult to work or split. It is used for furniture, interior finishing, siding, musical instruments, boxes, and crates. Occasionally it is used for butcher blocks.

One of the most important, but least recognized, problems of sycamores is that the fuzz on its leaves, fruits and young twigs can cause allergic reactions, including temporary blindness, if the branches are handled in pruning. That is why I have never pruned my sycamores! A less serious problem, for the tree not its caretaker, is the spring fungus, *anthracnose*. The fungus kills young leaves, although I have noticed that secondary shoots develop when the warmer summer weather dries the fungus. I have not seen the fungus defoliate any leaves on my two trees.

The sycamore tree across from Independence Hall in Philadelphia was germinated from a seed carried to the moon and back in 1971 by astronaut Stuart Roosa, a former Forest Service firefighter. Several of its sister seedlings, all germinated by the Forest Service upon Roosa's return to Earth, can be found in other locations around the country.

The sycamore genus is the only member of its plant family that has survived for over one million years, since the Cretaceous Period. It is a true elder among the tree tribes. I understand that in New Zealand, the government declared a river used by the Maori tribe Whanganui of the North Island to be a legal person that can sue if it is harmed. I ponder how we can give the sycamore similar legal status, to protect it for future generations.

Robinia pseudoacacia
Black Locust

The black locust is in the legume family, related to peas and beans. It grows in an upright, somewhat open habit, reaching fifty to seventy feet tall. In early summer, its pendulous displays of sweet-scented white flowers attract bees and butterflies. Its black and gray, or taupe, bark is deeply furrowed. The branches are brittle, breaking easily in the wind, accounting for the ragged, snaggy appearance of old locusts. The trees begin flowering at the age of ten to twelve years and seldom live more than one hundred years. The biggest black locust, topping out at 115 feet tall with a 124 foot spread, apparently grows in Michigan. I have been unable to validate its size nor its location. Where is it?

As a member of the legume family, *Robinia* produces its own nitrogen, making it reasonably self-sufficient in that it does not require fertilizer. Of course, it still appreciates mulching as all trees do. Black locust leaves have a feather-like appearance with short, paired spines flanking the leaf scars. The leaves turn a shade of gold and yellow in the fall but are not particularly striking nor beautiful. The prickles that arm the tree are not thorns. They are stipules, thorn-like appendages that grow on the trunk sprouting new branches. They can be sharp!

Locusts are monoecious, meaning they have staminate and pistillate flowers on the same tree. The flowers resemble pea blossoms and are arranged in drooping clusters. They are insect pollinated and produce the short, brown pods that hang on the tree until the following spring. Heavy seed crops are produced at one- to two-year intervals. Mourning doves, bobwhites, and other birds will eat the seeds.

On rainy days and at dusk, locusts leaves fold while the leaf itself droops from its stem, similar to the acacia. (The black locust is also known as a false acacia.) Botanists believe that this habit of "cuddling down" allows the trees to avoid excessive loss of moisture and heat. John Parkinson (1567-1650), English scientist, herbalist, botanist and author, wrote: "…each leaf folding itself double every evening upon sunne setting, and opening again the rising."

Locusts have a spreading root system and are cloning, making them useful for erosion control around beaches. The bacteria (*Rhizobium*) in its nitrogen filled root nodules enriches the soil. The tree is now naturalized over much of the United States.

Leaf "mining" or leaf "roller" moth caterpillars feed on locust leaves by rolling several leaflets together and then feeding inside. Beetles too make these characteristic mines on its leaflets. Other beetles, most notably the black and yellow lined longhorn beetle, burrow through the tree's bark into its sapwood, leaving long, winding tunnels which weaken the tree. Locusts often have elongated galls, which indicate larval feeding of the locust twig borer, another moth. My six locust trees are all healthy and without signs of any of these pests.

The Latin word *locusta* means both "lobster" and "locust" as in the insects. "Locusts with wild honey" were said to be the diet of John the Baptist when he was wandering in the wilderness. Botanists and Biblical scholars now believe that the "locusts" on which John the Baptist fed were really the pods of the carob tree. Is this why carob trees are also known as locust trees? Beats me. But the first settlers to Virginia noted the similarity of the tree they saw on the Atlantic shore to the carob/locust tree, and thus named it "black locust." Indeed, both trees are in the legume family, Fabaceae.

Locust tree wood is one of the strongest in North America. It shrinks little when drying, exceeding even hickory in stiffness. In 1607, the first English colonists made a permanent settlement on a little island in the James River, Virginia. Being mostly "well dressed" fortune hunters and lacking the skills of lumber jacks and carpenters, they made do with the surrounding trees when constructing their settlement. Mark Catesby, the British naturalist, visited Virginia a century after the founding of Jamestown and remarked: "Being obliged to run up with all the expedition possible such houses as might serve them to dwell in, till they could find leisure to build larger and convenient ones, they erected each of the little hovels on four only of these trees, ... the locust-tree of Virginia." Many of these posts are still standing! The durability of locust wood, even when in contact with the soil, allowed the settlers to survive in "hovels."

Commercially, locust wood is used for fence posts, railroad ties, tool handles, and insulator pins on utility poles. Except for the flowers, all parts of this tree contain the compounds robin, a phytotoxin, and robitin, a glycoside, poisonous to humans and most animals. These toxins can be used to produce a fungicide useful for treating and preserving wood. Indeed, the superiority of the locust wood used to construct United States warships during the war of 1812 is credited with their victory over the British Navy on Lake Champlain.

We lived at 1533 Chateaufort Place, Detroit, for over twenty years. Several *Robinia frisia*, a cultivar known as "honey locust," graced our courtyards. The trees' leaves, progressing from pale gold in the springtime, to green in summer, and then to golden-copper in the fall, were a sunny sight from urban windows.

Another unrelated tree with the same name of honey locust, (*Gleditsia triacanthos*), grows thorns in vicious clusters as long as a foot!

> *On numerous occasions, we drove to the Shakespeare Festival in Stratford, Ontario. Often, we packed a lunch to sit under the black locusts on an island in the Avon River, noting their zigzag branches.*

Mimosa or Silk Tree

Because of its delicate pink blossoms, don't assume that my mimosa tree is fragile or tropical. In fact, it survived a stretch of extremely cold weather, during the winter of 2017-18 when it was well below zero degrees for two weeks, and then grew back to its original height of about twenty-five feet. The mimosa is hardy to zone five or six, if sheltered from the frigid wind off of Lake Huron, as mine is.

The mimosa is native to Asia, where it is grown as an ornamental tree. It was introduced to the United States from Persia by the French botanist and explorer Andre Michaux in 1785.

The mimosa's fluffy blossoms appear on its wide-reaching branches in mid-summer, when other trees are looking tired and dry. Its leaves are doubly divided and of the finest texture. If you press them between your fingers, they will close or coil up to protect themselves as if physically stressed. The leaves eventually re-open and return to the original shape—amazing to me.

Are trees capable of learning? If so, where do they store what they have learned and how do they access the information? In the best-selling book, *The Hidden Life of trees,* Peter Wohlleben and other scientists are skeptical and banish such ideas of intelligent trees to the realm of fantasy.

Perhaps the mimosa is not intelligent, but, as Australian scientist, Dr. Monica Gagliano calls them, they are "sensitive plants." Gagliano deigned experiments whereby water would drip on the tree's foliage at regular intervals. At first, the "anxious" leaves closed immediately, but after a while, the tree leaves "learned" there was no danger of damage from the water droplets. After that, the leaves remained open despite the drops of water. Did the mimosa tree remember and apply the lessons learned, even without any further tests? Another resource from the University of Western Australia, "Move Over Elephants—Plants Have Memories Too," (University News, January 15, 2014), provides additional evidence that plants and trees can remember.

In the last twenty-five years, scientists have confirmed that plants and trees of the same species can communicate with each other by releasing pheromones or gases. In several studies, when one moth larva landed on a mature oak tree, the tree's leaves began producing bitter tannin, making it unappealing or even poisonous for the larva. What is astounding is that all the other oak trees nearby similarly changed the chemistry of their leaves, rendering them unappetizing as well.

In his book *The Hidden Life of Trees (2016)*, Peter Wohlleben describes the "underground social networks" of all trees as a constellation of fungi mycelial connecting the trees within the soil in a market exchange of carbon and nutrients. Amazing that mother trees recognize and "talk" with their kin, shaping future generations by gene regulation, defense chemistry and resilience in the forest community.

Is that anthropocentric or what? Should significant trees have legal standing? Or even civil rights? As Peter Wohlleben writes, think about it before you discard a good idea.

ALBIZIA julibrissin (MIMOSA-silk tree)

CERCIS CANADENSIS
Redbud or Judas Tree

Redbud has neither red buds nor red flowers but brightens the landscape in early spring while in full bloom. Its arching branches, including at ground level, are covered with pretty rose-pink blossoms as colorful as any shrub or tree. It is a beauty when its blossoms cheerfully open producing brilliant pink and purple colors. The flowers are unusual in that they are not restricted to the one-year twigs or spur branches; flower buds push through the bark of all but the very oldest and largest limbs. The subsequent dry brown seedpods, like pea pods, develop in clusters and persist through the winter.

The blossoms are harvested for food in Mexico, as they were in the Carolinas by early settlers. A passage in John Lawson's *History of North Carolina*, published in 1708, speaks of salads made of blossoms and eaten as a delicacy. I have read that early season butterflies visit the blossoms for their nectar and that the petals serve as a primary food source for the larvae of the ephemeral flutter-by, Henry's Elfin (*Callophrys henrici*). However, I have never seen nor discovered larvae or butterflies on my redbud.

The redbud is an excellent residential garden tree because it adapts to most soils and growing conditions, and is shade tolerant. It grows up to ten feet tall and can be trimmed.

Judas tree is an older name, transferred to the United States species from the Mediterranean in accordance with the belief or superstition that it was the tree from which Judas Iscariot hanged himself after he betrayed Jesus. Wherefore its flowers and blossoms which were formerly "white" turned "red" with shame and/or blood. Guilty as charged.

Castor Aralia

Castor aralia is in the ginseng family, and is dominant in Japan, China, Korea, and the Russian Far East. Although related to the poisonous castor bean plant, *Ricinus communis*, it is a distinct, one of a kind species. Its scientific name comes from the Greek *kalos* meaning "beautiful" and *panakes* meaning "healing." *Septemlobus* is Latin for "seven lobes," referring to the leaves. (The Classical languages, Greek and Latin, are still taught in many high schools, colleges and universities—hurrah!) You may guess from its name that it is valued for the ethnopharmacology of its leaves, bark and roots.

Charles Sprague Sargent (1841-1927), botanist and director of Arnold Arboretum, Harvard University, was so intrigued by the plant, that he went to Japan in 1892 to collect its seeds. Today, two trees grace the permanent collection at the Arboretum on the eastern bank of Rehder Pond. According to our guide when we visited the Arboretum, the trees are from the seeds that Sargent collected.

The tree has huge leaves, about seven inches long, that are attached to the branch by long stems or petioles. The lobed leaves turn brilliant greenish yellow in autumn. The tree is deciduous, and typically grows to about ninety or one hundred feet tall with a trunk diameter of about a yard. I have a beautiful castor aralia on the northern boundary of our driveway. I find its winter frame really distinctive. Its few thick forked twigs reach as if yearning to write on the sky. It brightens a bleak winter day.

The tree is armed with stout prickles that protrude from the thick bark which becomes deeply furrowed with age. Its white flowers blossom in August and September, providing nectar for pollinators. With successful pollination, the tree will yield abundant blue-black fruits that remain well into winter. I often see birds eating the berries from my tree, but most sources say that the berries are inedible! Toxic? I guess it depends.

Castor aralia apparently has the ability to give rise to ferocious suckers, but I am still waiting, as I'm a sucker for trees! Is this "suckering" habit invasive? I don't let that bother me as I marvel over my unique thriving specimen. It looks like I have a tropical tree growing.

Liriodendron tulipifer

Tulip Tree

The two tulip trees on my property are among my most favorite. I planted them years ago after visiting the Arnold Arboretum at Harvard University. Knowing my interest in trees, my friend John McCauliff, Florence Mosqueda's husband, proudly took me to "the" Arboretum. That is where I first saw a tulip tree. I gaped. It was one of the tallest natives I had ever seen, topping out at about 150 feet.

The tulip tree is the king of the Magnolia family, the tallest hardwood in North America. In Southern Appalachia, old forest growth trees attain superb dimensions, not only of height, but of trunk girth—eight to ten feet in diameter clear of branches. The tree maintains its liveliness and continues with swift growth well into maturity because it is marvelously free of disease and decay.

The leaves look as if they have "chopped-off" ends and are unlike any other tree leaf in shape. They wear remarkably well, having few insect foragers, and flutter in the breeze because of their long, angled leafstalks. Their emergence in the spring is unique. From terminal buds shaped like duck-bills successions of bills uncurl and unfold, revealing a marvel of leaf engineering. Worthy of a "Wow!" The unusually shaped leaves are bright green and turn brilliant yellow in fall. Its bark has vertical, crosscut fissures likening to a series of parallel mountain ridges with deep gullies in their sides.

In late spring, the tree's goblet-shaped flowers open. The petals are greenish yellow and have orange blotches at the base, looking much the same as tulips. Regrettably the tree bears these blooms too high for close inspection. Only with binoculars can the details be seen. Hummingbirds relish the nectar of the flowers, as do bees for making honey. (I have not tasted tulip tree honey.)

Fossils of various species of the tulip tree date from the Upper Cretaceous period, about seventy million to one hundred million years ago, but all species, except for two, were wiped out by the Pleistocene glaciation, one in Eastern China and one in the Eastern United States.

In 1972, in celebration of the centenary of its founding, the Arnold Arboretum developed several magnolia cultivars. One is the *Magnolia stellata* "Centennial Star." Other hybrids abound. Breeders in Japan, China and New Zealand have sought different colors, larger flowers and more robust smaller trees to withstand frosts.

The Joyce Kilmer Memorial Forest, located in the Nantahala National Forest at the western end of North Carolina, hosts a very impressive grove of tulip trees. A remnant of our natural heritage, these dozens of straight massive tulip trees, with trunks as thick as farm silos, provide an inspiring glimpse of what used to be the "norm."

Pioneers, settlers and farmers fed the aromatic twigs of the young trees to livestock. The inner bark of the roots and trunk, intensely acrid and bitter, is the source of alkaloid tulipiferine, a heart stimulant. Native Americans used powdered bark and seeds as a remedy for worms. They fashioned canoes from the trunk. History records that Daniel Boone (1734-1829) hollowed out a single log to build a canoe sixty feet long. When his fortunes were low in Kentucky, he piled his family and belongings into the canoe and sailed away down the Ohio River into Spanish territory. He died in Missouri. The light and soft wood is used commercially for paneling, interior and exterior trim, veneers, and is the favorite material for hat blocks since it does not absorb moisture.

The tulip tree is the state tree of Indiana, Tennessee, Kentucky, and North Carolina, but thrives in Michigan—as my two trees can testify. I hope they can be more widely planted and admired for their unique attributes, history and beauty.

Pseudotsuga menziesii
Douglas Fir

Undoubtedly, at least as I write this chapter, my favorite tree is the Douglas fir, which can be spelled as a singular species Douglasfir. The Douglasfir belongs to the family of Pinaceae, which also includes the pines – Pinus; the firs – Abies; and the spruces – APicea. The Douglas fir is neither a fir nor a *Tsuga* hemlock but is uniquely named a *Pseudotsuga*. It grows along the California Pacific coast right up to British Columbia.

David Douglas (1799–1834) was a Scottish botanist and explorer who died under mysterious circumstances while climbing Mauna Kea in Hawaii at the age of 35. He fell into a pit trap and then apparently was crushed by a bull that fell into the trap after him. He was last seen at the hut of Englishman Edward "Ned" Gurney, a bullock hunter and escaped convict. Hmmm? Douglas was buried in an unmarked grave near Mission House, Honolulu.

At the age of 11, Douglas was employed as an apprentice gardener at Scone Palace. He attended college in Perth and then the University of Glasgow, eventually working at the university's botanical gardens. Because of his prodigious knowledge, he was nominated to join the Royal Horticultural Society of London. During his career, he made three trips to North America on plant-hunting expeditions, introducing at least twelve, if not more, notable species of trees, predominantly pines, spruces and firs. Today, over eighty species of plants, trees, and animals have the designation *douglassi* in their scientific names.

The Douglasfir's scientific name *Pseudotsuga menziesii* honors a rival botanist, Scottish surgeon and naturalist Archibald Menzies (1754–1842), who reached the summit of his career in 1790, forty years before David Douglas. Menzies accompanied Captain George Vancouver (the namesake of the Canadian city) on his voyage around the world.

I planted six Douglasfirs on our property. I also planted two in New Britain; one in Walnut Hill Park shortly before we left Connecticut in 2000, and one at our old home, 5 Elbridge Road, in 1993, after tornadic winds toppled a maple into our neighbor's house!

We built our new home using Douglasfir exclusively for the walls and ceiling on the first and second floors, making up about 2,658 square feet of wood. Our home is a total of 5,088 square feet; the first floor is 2,224 square feet, the second floor is 640 square feet, the lower level or finished basement is 1,724 square feet, and the pool and sauna area is five hundred square feet.

There is a flagpole in Kew Gardens, London, a UNESCO World Heritage side, more than sixty meters (over 196 feet) tall, sawed straight as a die from a single trunk of Douglass fir!

> *When we visited our granddaughter, Andy, in British Columbia (she is a graduate of UBC) we saw huge trees. It was the summer of 2018 and during that trip, we were also able to visit Aunt Lucia A. Santos Calaguas, Sally's father's sister. We stayed with Auntie Lucinda's son, Ray Calaguas and his wife, Myline and their son, Gerard. We explored the province together for two weeks, visiting Native villages and of course admiring the majestic western red cedars, grand firs, and Sitka spruces.*

The cones of the Douglas fir act as flowers in the reproductive life of the tree, producing very large amounts of pollen grain every spring—not too popular with allergy sufferers or swimmers in Lake Huron when it washes up to the shore. But the pollen coats the tree's sperm cells too, protecting them as the cells move from the stamen of one cone, or tree flower, to the pistil of the next flower. The tree's male flowers produce prodigious amounts of pollen to fertilize the tree's female flowers, ensuring reproduction. The complexity, not eroticism, of what's happening when fertilization occurs inside a tree flower or cone is amazing! A vivid description of fertilization appears in David Suzuki and Wayne Grady's book, *Tree: A Life Story*:

> The female cone of the Douglass-fir remains receptive to male pollen grains for twenty days, until the end of April. Once a pollen grain has slipped down the smooth surface of the seed cone bracts, it becomes enmeshed in the small sticky hairs at the tip of the female ovule. For two months it luxuriates on this pubic patch while the ovule's labia swell around it; slowly the oval engulfs the grain, which sinks into it like a croquet ball into a soft, silken pillow.

It takes just one pollen grain penetrating the nucleus of one ovule in one Douglas-fir to produce a new cone and perhaps a tree. Miraculous how love conquers all!

PINUS

The Pines

Pinus, the pines, is the biggest of the three conifer genera (Abies, the firs and Picea, the spruces being the other two) with 109 known species. It is also the oldest; pines have been growing in Europe since the Cretaceous period, about sixty million years ago. They range from the tropics to the tundra, from the mountains to the shining sea. From towering ponderosa pine to dwarf shrubs, they are a unique attribute to any garden simply for their ornamental value.

Most pines will adapt to poor soils, extending their roots via the (fungi) mycorrhizae. Witness the pines that self-seeded on our sandy beach! When the Europeans settled on Cape Cod in the wake of the earlier Pilgrims who had cut down the pine forests, they assumed there would be rich soil beneath, but they found only sand dunes, totally unsuitable for growing wheat. They could not plant, nor could they fish the teeming cod from the sea for want of a fishhook. They nearly starved!

Pinus resimosa (Red Pine)

The red pine, *Pinus resimosa* is native to North America. The oldest and largest groves of red pine grow in the Great Lakes region. At maturity, the red pine reaches fifty to seventy feet with a trunk diameter of two to three feet. They have smooth, symmetrical, two to two and one half inch cones, of a light chestnut-brown color. In contrast, white pines have drooping, four to eight inches long cones of a light reddish brown color. Neither cone has prickles. Red pine has long been the companion to the graceful white pine "queen of the forest." Like a consort to a queen, it is seldom mentioned or remarked upon. Its rugged, red-brown bark has narrow furrows, broad ridges, and loose scales. Red pines have two needles per cluster. The needles are unique in that they fracture or break completely when bent in two.

The beautiful red pine on the north property line near our house started growing about 2001. It has been damaged several times over the years by northeast gale blizzards and ice storms. Ice has broken several apical branches when the winds have piled huge snow drifts over the top of the tree! It is strong and regal, withstanding the elements because it sports triple leaders.

Pinus nigra (Black Pine or Austrian Pine)

The red pine is often confused with the black or Austrian pine, introduced from Europe. The black pine is somewhat stouter, and its less shiny needles do not fracture or break when bent in two. Its cones have prickles (on the cone scales) and its bark is a gray-black color. The winter twigs of the Austrian pine are yellowish brown, whereas those of the red pine are bright red. In my experience as a master gardener, the Austrian pine is susceptible to fungi, but is tolerant of air pollutants, and is therefore often planted on urban streets.

Pinus banksiana (Jack pine)

Pinus banksiana or Jack pines line our driveway. This beautifully shaped pine makes a lovely Christmas tree. It bears separate staminate (filament and anther) and pistillate (stigma and ovary) and therefore is dioecious, having separate male and female trees. Its pinecones, the smallest of all pines, are deep rich purple. Its needles are soft light green.

Jack pines thrive in North America and, similar to aspens, have an ability to bounce back after fire, which inevitably strikes the boreal forest sooner or later. If the ground is frozen or wet during fire, the Jack pine's roots will survive. But even if there is fire under dry conditions, Jack pine grow back rapidly drawing upon their especially vast root systems.

But it is the cones and seeds of the Jack pine that are particularly adapted to fire. The cones are as tough as nails; their scales tightly bound together with a type of resinous glue. Only the red squirrel can attack the cones, although they prefer the easier to access, fleshier meat of spruce cones. The cones can persist for years, as Colin Tudge indicates in his book, *The Secret Life of Trees*, "…cones that were more than twenty years old were able to germinate." The cones do not open until there is fire. It takes heat of fifty degrees Celsius to melt the resin, or hydrocarbon secretion, that locks the scales together. But the Jack pine employs another survival technique, about 10 percent of the cones will open by the warmth of the sun. I have seen this happen with my trees. It is a mixed survival strategy, dependent on both fire and the sun. Geneticists call this process a "balanced polymorphism" developed by the scrappy Jack pine as it adapted to the climate of the Great Lakes states.

Western Pines

The western pines are in a different league altogether. In size, vigor, and variety the western pines are the world champions. The western pines include the *Pinus lambertiana* aka sugar pine, *Pinus ponderosa*, *Pinus monticola* aka western white pine, *Pinus jeffreyi*, *Pinus aristata* aka bristlecone pine, *Pinus contorta* aka lodgepole pine, *Pinus radiata* aka Monterey pine, *Pinus torretana* aka the Torrey pine, *Pinus cembroides* aka the piñon pine, *Pinus spatula* aka jelecote or spreading-leaf pine, *Pinus ayacahuite* aka Mexican white pine, the *Pinus muricata* aka the bishop pine, and *Pinus coulteri*. David Douglas, exploring the seaward slopes of the Sierras for a time in 1820, wrote in a report: "You will begin to think I manufacture pines at my pleasure."

With over one hundred species of pines, it is hard to pick a favorite. But, my heart belongs to the bristlecone pine, which grows in the Rocky Mountains and attains the height of only six to seven feet in twenty years! The bristlecone pine grows infinitesimally slowly because of its intensely harsh living conditions. Talk about endurance, longevity, and stinginess. Bristlecone pines in a protected area of the White Mountains of California may be over 3,000 years old. Because of the arid desert atmosphere, the trees' dead limbs do not rot. Bristlecone pines are super-sensitive rain gauges. Tree-ring width in dry regions can provide an approximation of total rainfall over a growth cycle. The rings of the bristlecone pine are microscopically narrow, 1,100 rings in the space of five inches.

The University of Arizona, Laboratory of Tree-Ring Research Center, has developed a technique for matching samples of wood from living and dead trees, even broken-off bits lying on the desert floor, to build up and model a continuous series of rings from which to document the rainfall. The laboratory expects eventually to push the records back to 10,000 years of weather, back centuries when the last ice age was in retreat.

Of course, wood from any tree, living or dead, can be tested by the carbon-14 method, which holds good for the last 3,500 years. But with trees this old, the methods have to change. We will wait and see!

None of the western pines grow well in Michigan. I planted a bristlecone pine in the west thicket, and it was doing alright but lived only about twelve or fifteen years. It reached a height of only about twelve inches, and never produced cones. I have not replaced it.

I also have two *coulteri* pinecones, named after the Irish physician Thomas Coultier (1793-1843), botanist and explorer. Pearl Stavers, now deceased, brought them as souvenirs for us from her many trips to California to visit family. It is now illegal to take the giant cones out of California! I keep them indoors and display them on our stairs landing. Each cone can weigh up to five pounds and are named "widow makers" because they can kill you!

Other pines I have planted on my property are shrubby Mugo pines on the south of the property near Mo and Jane's home, the scrub tree *Pinus virginiana* fenced in the west thicket, and *Pinus koraiensis* or Korean pine in the west thicket. (Also, although not a *Pinus*, but in the same Pinales family, I have an *Araucaria heterophylla* or Norfolk Island pine growing potted inside our home.)

PINUS STROBUS

White Pine

Pinus strobus, eastern white pine, is the most majestic conifer in the Great Lakes regions.

Our home is nestled between five huge white pines all planted in the mid-fifties by Edward and Mary Weitoff on the highest elevation of the property. We and my parents bought the cottage with all its furnishings from them when they moved to Florida after Mr. Weitoff's retirement from Kroger's in 1977. The cottage was small, built on a cement floor and heated only with a liquid propane tank and fireplace. We negotiated a land contract for $49,000 with a 6 percent interest rate. We put just about 10 percent down, $4,500. We paid off the balance owed in the amount of $9,000 on September 4, 1988, and my folks signed the deed over to us. At the time, I was CEO of Southwest Solutions (a comprehensive mental health center) and Sally was practicing medicine as a certified Physician's Assistant at the Detroit Medical Center. The purchase was initially made as an investment to meet the obligations for three children to go to college, but…they merited scholarships, worked while in college and borrowed low interest loans and we still have the property!

I retired in 1999, and after about a year of planning, in 2000, Sally and I began to build our "dream" home. I become a licensed builder and contractor because, as a contractor, as long as you jump through the right hoops and pay $660 per annum, you're entitled to a thirty-three and a third percent discount on all building supplies, lumber and materials. We salvaged and gave away everything we could: plumbing, insulation, bathroom fixtures, southern knotty pine paneling, and furniture, giving it all to friends in the county, and demolished the cottage. We received our occupancy permit in May 2001, after thirteen months of construction, just months before 9/11.

I am embarrassed to reveal how little I knew before I embarked on this book, especially about the white pine! I have always admired the elegance of the white pines by our house, with their pagoda-like outlines against the skyline, and I have personally marked their propensity for rapid growth. But that was the limit of my awareness or knowledge, other than toying with their cones, getting my fingers sticky with sap. Thoreau wrote: "It is the stickiest work I ever did."

White pines are the only pines with five needles to each cluster. The needles function like leaves and perform photosynthesis all year long, exchanging carbon dioxide, oxygen, and water vapor with the air in a process called transpiration. White pine needles are rich in vitamins A and C. They contain five times as much vitamin C as an equal weight of lemons. Native Americans chopped the pine's spring needles and steeped them for tea to be taken for coughs and colds as an expectorant. The inner bark could also be used as a poultice for sores and wounds.

The white pine's female "flowers" are hard to see, but with binoculars (a mature white pine grows to about 150 feet), you can observe the finger-like projections emerging from the tops of new shoots that grow in the pine's upper canopy. They are about a tiny quarter inch long. The small cones look like golden-green buds with red, fleshy scalloped scales. Wind carries pollen from the male cones to the immature female cones. The female cones' scales spread apart to receive the pollen then close, sealing the cones. By the end of the second summer, the female cones will have matured into bullet-like cones, three-quarters to an inch and a half long. This reproductive process takes two years, from flowers to seeds. It is a miracle that the white pine knows what to do and can repeat it with exactitude.

On each cone, there are usually two seeds lodged behind each scale. The seeds are tiny, only about one-fourth inch long, with a wing of about three-fourth inch long. It is surprising to me how far a seed with one wing will fly. Wind turns the seeds into gyroscopes with single blade propellers. The strong wind off the Lake can carry the seeds for miles to leeward. Caught in a back eddy, I have stood and watched seeds whirling over our home and then in a sudden lull, spin into the grass, hoping to germinate. The seeds are edible, but too hard to harvest unless you're a squirrel. Numerous songbirds, small animals, and insects feast on the seeds and spring needles.

Donald Peattie, in his classic book *A Natural History of Trees,* wrote about "aboriginal" New England, with its pristine white pine forests: "When the male flowers bloomed in these illimitable pineries, thousands of miles of forest aisle were swept with golden smoke of this reckless fertility, and great storms of pollen were swept from the primal shores far sea and to the superstitious sailors seemed to be raining brimstone on the deck."

Have you smelled or tasted pine needles? The piney odor is due to chemical compounds called terpenes. Terpenes are abundant in conifer resin, and when a tree's bark is damaged, the resin flows out and then hardens to protect the tree from insects, beetles, and fungal pathogens. Turpentine is made from pine resin and is used as a curative, a flavoring, a fragrance and cleaning or paint solvents. My Dad, who worked as a mechanic, used the solvent powers of turpentine to remove grease from his hands.

The white pine is unrivaled as a timber producing tree. It played a momentous role in the life and history of America… and Britain. Fleets of ships with their tall, straight, Eastern white pine masts sailed swiftly around the world. As early as 1605, Captain George Weymouth of the British navy, sailed a Maine river and gazed at the enormous white pines. He took specimen logs for "mast-wood," and seedlings and seeds back to England, but the pines never proved adaptable to the English climate. Exploitation began immediately and the importation of white pine from America allowed the British to rule the seas for centuries! No wood light enough, strong enough, or straight enough for masting was grown in Europe, so England remained mistress of the seas, forever at war with other navies, whether it be Prussia, Russia, Sweden or Danes. The British thereby grew rich and occupied a position of political power commensurate with their wealth.

Starting with the colonists, people have laid waste to the white pine forests, including those in Michigan. Colonists viewed themselves as speculators or exploiters of vast impregnable wilderness, with all its resources, despite the thousands or millions of Native Americans or

"Indians" that inhabited the land, and whom they considered cruel savages. There were many conflicts between the colonists and Native Americans, such as the Pequot War (1636-1638); the Beaver Wars (16401701); King Philip War aka Metacomet's War (1675-1676); and others.

Historians document and write about the fact that the white pine was one of the chief economic and psychological factors in the gathering storm of the American Revolution. King George I issued a decree to reserve the grandest specimens of trees, especially the white pine because of its specific characteristics, for the Royal Navy. The "Crown Lands" or royal domain were all used in the Empire's battles against Spain, Holland and France, all at their own expense.

By the late 1800s, as the number of river lumber mills expanded, the white pine forests were so mercilessly exploited that the United States government by necessity passed the country's first forest conservation laws. New England had already lost about 70 percent of its forests.

It is worth a weekend to visit Hartwick Pines State Park, 4216 Ranger Road, Grayling, Michigan, to visit the museum, yes, but especially the park's forest of old growth white pines.

Now you know why white pines merit a special chapter. It would take a lifetime of study to enumerate this special pine's various uses, qualities, and attributes!

Pinus contorta

Lodgepole Pine

At the end of the Wisconsin Ice Age, about eleven thousand years ago, our climate changed dramatically, from subarctic to temperate. A temperate climate, with its mild, wet winters and dry summers, allows deciduous and conifer forests to thrive. Among the first species to establish itself to this new climate was the lodgepole pine, dominating the landscape of the West Coast. The Douglasfirs and other species associated with the miraculous habitats and temperate climes soon joined them. These temperate rain forests support the greatest biomass per hectare of any ecosystem on Earth.

The lodgepole pine gets its name because the Native Americans utilized poles of *Pinus contorta* wood to support their dwellings. The trees are primarily located in the Cascades but will grow elsewhere because they are environmentally tolerant. The lodgepole pine has dense foliage with striking red tips that make it look as if it is flowering. The pine can reach about 150 feet, and matures with cones within twelve to twenty months. Its needles, four to eight inches long, are serrated. The cones are serotinous, which means they remain closed, for up to seventy-five years, if there is no fire to disperse the seeds. Although, without fire, the closed cones will eventually drop from the tree, decompose and then release their seeds. The cones are "sessile" meaning they are attached to the branch without a stem.

Have you ever tasted or smelled the bark? It reminds me of vanilla or butterscotch, rather pleasant.

It is rather curious to me that a lodgepole pine can develop needles, buds, and cones within two years. I have puzzled over this. A plant's hormones, known as auxins, are needed to initiate rapid cell growth. A tree's auxins travel down the trunk in the phloem, but unlike other nutrients being transported, the auxins concentrate in specific areas of the pine, such as the cones. The auxins do not distribute themselves equally into the cells of either the roots or the buds, each of which needs auxins to grow. Auxins concentrate in the roots because of gravity, but how do they get to the plumule or embryo buds, encouraging them to grow? But the cells need more than auxins to develop, which gives me a good answer, the growth of the lodgepole, as most other plants, depends on sunlight. Although lower concentrations of auxins affect the growth of the plumule or embryo buds, with a lot of sun, a lodgepole seedling, with its roots growing rapidly downward will still raise its buds up to the sun.

Commercially, lodgepole pines are sold as pressed treated lumber for construction and furniture. The lodgepole pine is the official tree of the Province of Alberta, an emblem of its arboreal forest.

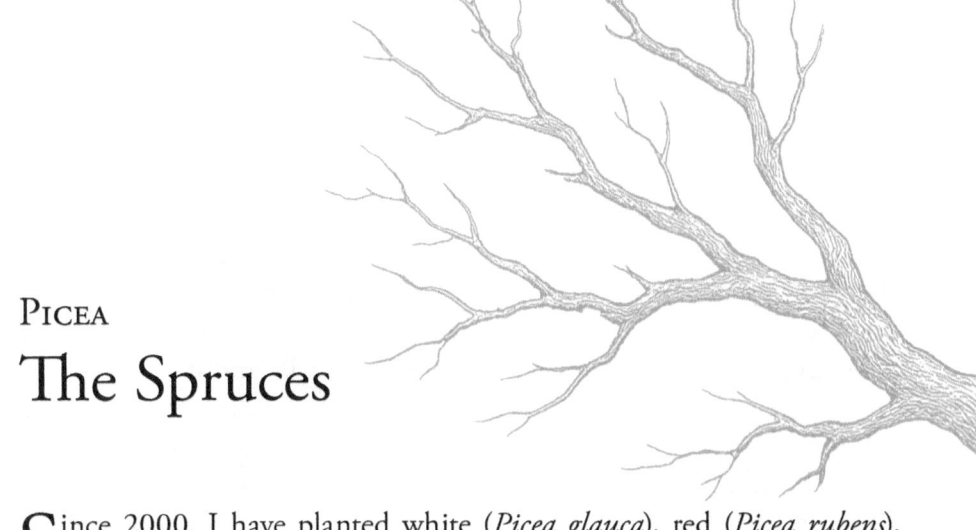

PICEA
The Spruces

Since 2000, I have planted white (*Picea glauca*), red (*Picea rubens*), black (*Picea mariana*) and many other spruces that I have been unable to classify. Although there are about forty species of spruce growing in North America – from the Great Lakes up through the boreal forest and as far south as the mountain tops of the Great Smokies – I initially focused only on these three species, white, red and black spruces.

I planted four white spruce and two red spruce (along with a Korean fir) on the property line shared with our previous neighbors, Mo and Jane Felling. In the west section of our property, I have planted a pyramidal black spruce, which can be recognized by its gorgeous crimson and light maroon cones. As one of my first ventures beyond these three species, I planted a dwarf-drooping Norway spruce (*Picea abies*) in our courtyard in 2010.

More recently, in appreciation for our daughter-in-law Patty Hogan, I planted a striking ornamental *Picea abies* in Mark and Patty's front yard in Ann Arbor. Patty volunteered as my healthcare agent and chauffeur, managing my hospital stays and doctor's appointments during my 15-month siege with cancer. Our other "five" children stepped up when she needed to pass the baton. I chose the Norway spruce because Patty and Mark spent a semester in Bergen, Norway, on a Fulbright Scholar sabbatical shortly after my cancer went into remission, from August through December 2019.

Needles often get less attention than leaves. Needles are "modified" leaves and perform the same functions of leaves; in fact, because they are evergreen, through photosynthesis, they manufacture food for trees all year. Other leafy or needle functions include cell respiration and transpiration, i.e., exchanging carbon dioxide, oxygen and water vapor with the air. Several botanists and biology scientists claim that needles evolved to help snow sift to the ground instead of accumulating on the branches and breaking them.

Guiding visitors through many of my one hundred trees, many ask how to distinguish fir needles from spruce needles. I tear off a few needles from a spruce, round in cross section, and tell them to roll them between thumb and finger; softer fir needles are flat and they won't roll.

Hugh Johnson, British author of *The World of Trees*, gives us another simple test to determine whether a tree is a fir or a spruce. "Pull a living needle off a twig. If it leaves a neat round mark, a slight dent, it is fir: if a little piece of bark comes too, leaving a torn scar, it is a spruce." (His book has become a valuable resource, providing the most reliable information, with color photographs and other treasures, that I've discovered in my twenty years of planting trees. I have also discovered what trees will not grow in twenty years.) It is also interesting to note that when spruce needles fall naturally, minute pegs which form on their bases stay on the twig, making it sharp and rough to the touch. Whereas fir twigs and branches are peg-less, and consequently smooth.

A friend of mine from Kaleva, Michigan, Andrew Pihl, a Finn, had acres of trees and could identify them by the wind whistling through their leaves and needles. It is still a mystery to me. He taught me to listen to pines, spruce, balsam, hemlock, maple, Jack pine, …and to wait and wonder what they're saying! The needles and leaves comb and voice the winds.

Conifers, including spruces, produce quite different male and female cones on the same tree. If you can see a cone's woody structures, an archetypal pinecone, it is a female cone in which the tree's seeds develop. These cones remain on the tree for at least a year, and some persist for several years up to a decade. Their orientation to the branch varies. Female cones of the spruce hang down and female cones of the fir point up. It took me years to recognize male cones because they are not woody and do not "look" like pinecones. Male cones, often referred to as pollen cones, are smaller and stubbier than female cones, and are simpler in structure and much more numerous. Compared to female seed cones, male pollen cones are relatively short-lived, falling from the tree and quickly deteriorating as soon as they release their pollen. The male cones occur in clusters and at maturity, look like conglomerations of swollen, pollen-coated Q-tips. If you have ever noticed these structures on pines and wondered why they never developed into "real" pinecones, it is because they are the tree's male pollen cones, not its female seed cones.

Identifying the species of spruce is more difficult, and I have often been stumped because their needles, flowers and bark look alike. The species are distinguished in part by the size of the cones: the white spruce's cones are the largest at two inches long and have a pale green color tinged with red; the red spruce's cones can be from a quarter inch to two inches long and are shiny with a reddish color; and the black spruce has the smallest cones, which can be a quarter inch to no more than an inch and a half long, and have a gray-brown maroon color.

Every Lutheran knows (or should know) Luther's dates (14831546), especially because relatively recently, in 2017, we celebrated the five hundred year anniversary of his nailing the ninety-five theses to the church door in Wittenberg. But do you know the dates of Jacques Cartier, the first European to explore the North American interior, claiming and mapping eastern regions of Canada for France?

Jacques Cartier (1491-1557) was a contemporary of Luther. He saw his first white spruce in the autumn of 1535, as he sailed the Saguenay River, exploring the Saint Lawrence river basin. In the ship's log he recorded these words: "… and the finest trees of the world, to wit oaks, elms, walnuts, cedars, spruces, ash trees, willows and wild vines."

White spruce is most commonly used to make paper pulp, which is the chief reason for the disappearance of the great stands of virgin spruce, both white and red, throughout North America. It takes tons of water and power to turn out the morning newspapers.

One precious quality of the spruce is its *resonance,* which is superior to that of metal because it enriches and softens tones. Because spruce is generally of a uniform texture, free of defects and irregularities of grain, it is the preferred material for guitars, mandolins, cellos, violins, organ pipes, and sound boards for pianos and harps. The wood actually becomes more and more elastic with constant vibration. Old violins are truly aged in music. However, even the finest instruments, if neglected, stiffen up again.

The fiddle of Paganini, after lying in the museum in native Genoa, was found in fifty years to be a ruin so far as tone was concerned.

— Donald Peattie in *A Natural History of Trees*

White Spruce (Picea glauca)

There are large stands of red spruce in the White Mountains of New Hampshire. At the peak of Mount Washington, 6,288.2 feet above sea-level, one can encounter erratic weather patterns, with the highest recorded wind speed of 231 mph on April 12, 1934. It is no surprise that after experimenting with various species of wood, the Wright brothers settled on red spruce, with its strength and flexibility, for their initial flight.

The black spruce is my favorite spruce because of its curious forms and shapes—sculptured to its environs, adapting to natural forces. Sally and I visited the headwaters of the Mississippi River when we travelled to Macalester College for Sally's 50th reunion in 2007. It was there, on those swampy headwaters, where Sally and I marveled at the black spruce growing on the detritus of aquatic plants, sedges and sphagnum moss, life and death together. We visited that spot, with a riverine flowing south and where a Roman Catholic children's camp was located, after the wedding of Jon Dumpys and Stacy Jutala. During that same trip we explored Lake Itasca, the Mississippi River's primary source, the Red River of the North, which flows into Lake Winnipeg, as well as the St. Louis River, which flows into Lake Superior. There we discovered the many ill-drained ponds and lakes which were glaciated hundreds of years ago, and which now are full of floating islands upon which spruce grow without contact with mineral rich soil. These muskeg trees will bear cones when still only two or three feet in height, which may represent many years of growth. Cone bearing branches at the top of the small tree, crowded near the top, may be the tree's only living branches, the trunk below destitute of branches. Although this will only occur if "unshaded and growing far from other trees," according to Donald Culross Peattie, in his book: *A Natural History of Trees*. He continues: "These dense tufts of dark branches like plumes upon poles present a strange spectacle to the traveler who for the first time crosses the larger muskegs ...".

In addition to the three species of spruce, white, red, and black, I have planted several other varieties, including the *Picea abies* or Norway spruce; the *Engelmannii* or Engelmann spruce, which is similar to the Colorado blue spruce but has softer needles; *Likiangensis* or Likiang from China, which has bright purplish red young cones and is no stranger to heat and drought – in twenty years it can eventually reach fifty feet tall and twenty-five feet wide—just beautiful; *Omorika* or Serbian; and *Pungens*, also known as Colorado blue.

> *In 1985, the elder son of Dr. J. Lawrence and Charlotte Hill, John, died in a tragic skiing accident in British Columbia. His cremains were scattered on Mount Baldy, Colorado, where he owned a condo in Breckenridge. To memorialize his death, I transplanted an Engelmann spruce sapling on the north of our driveway where it is thriving. Our families travelled together to Alaska for one month in 1981 to relive the years when Larry and I hitch-hiked to Alaska during summers when we were students at Ohio Wesleyan University, Delaware, Ohio from 1953 to 1957. Great adventures and memories! (And we earned our tuition, room and board for OWU from our work in Alaska.)*

I have also planted dwarf spruces, such as *conica*, a dwarf Alberta spruce; *glauca*, a dwarf white spruce; and *sitchensis*, a dwarf Sitka spruce – in containers in our home.

Likiang spruce cones

I planted a Serbian spruce in the grove in the west end of our property near M-25 when President William Clinton had the warring parties sign the peace accords in Dayton, Ohio in 2001. The Yugoslav

Wars and ethnic conflicts, 1991-2001, involved Slovenia, Croatia, Bosnia and Herzegovina, Serbia, Montenegro, Kosovo and the Republic of Macedonia.

The Serbian spruce has beautiful arching branches and cascading bicolor foliage. Pyramidal when young, it becomes spike-like with maturity.

Picea pungens or Colorado blue spruce is the all-time winner of landscaping awards because of the unrivaled beauty of its prickly needles which become powder blue. It grows twenty feet in only twenty years, surviving in most soil conditions.

Picea glauca "albertiana" or dwarf Alberta spruce, was discovered in 1904 at the Lake Laggan train station in Alberta by Alfred Rehder and John G. Jack, agents for the Arnold Arboretum of Harvard University. Their studies established the tree as a naturally-occurring mutant of white spruce, rarely producing cones. In 1913, on the sesquicentennial of Rehder's birth (1863-1949), Harvard published the book, *Life Remembered in Plants*, to honor the taxonomist and scholar. You can confer Rehder's book *Manual of Cultivated Trees and Shrubs*, referred to as a botanist's bible, for detailed information on most all species.

White Spruce Cones

ABIES

The Firs

The word "abies" is derived from the Latin *abeo*, meaning "up-reaching" or "ascendant." There are about forty-eight to fifty species of firs worldwide, and they inhabit uplands from temperate to extreme northern cold zones, thriving between elevations of 2,500 to 4,000 feet. North America has nine of the firs, two in the east and seven in the west. The eastern species, the balsam and the Fraser firs, are smaller than the seven species in the west.

Balsam fir, known for its woodsy scent, is beautifully colored with green or blue-green needles, purple upright cones, about two to four inches in length, and rich brown bark. Its seeds fly through the woods on bright wings, a visible and a viable food source to squirrel, grouse, pine mice as well as moose and deer. It is adaptable and grows rapidly, which, along with its fertility, allows it to survive. Balsam, with a dense, pointed silhouette is the arboreal emblem of New Brunswick.

Balsams are monoecious with both male and female cones on the topmost branches of a single tree. The purple cones are ornamented by big pale yellow-green bracts with toothed margins that turn back over the scales.

A. balsamea is quite sensuous, exuding scented gum from every pore. Its bark carries blisters of clear, aromatic resin, as does its roots. Crush its needles and your hands are coated with delicious glue! President Roosevelt planted balsams at Hyde Park, New York because of their beauty and fragrance. This same resin is used in the manufacture of varnish, which has a familiar aroma if you have ever bought a balsam

Christmas tree. Unfortunately, because of the resin blisters under its bark, the tree will ignite into a blazing torch in the event of fire.

The resin can be used as wound plaster and waterproof cement. Native Americans also used it as a headache remedy. If mixed with bear grease, it also served as a hair dressing. Until the invention of modern adhesives, the resin was employed in various laboratories to mount microscopic specimens. Its current main economic value lies in Christmas; about thirty percent of all balsam trees are sold for the holidays.

The balsam fir has flat, not round, unstilted needles with two white stripes on their undersides, really beautiful. The needles are spirally arranged around the twig with a broad circular base and remain on the tree for about four years. However, I quickly discovered that the deer love the needles more than I do; I ended up having to fence our fast-growing fir after its apical shoot, the main central stem and tip of the tree, was totally devoured. Luckily, the plant hormone, auxin, eventually encouraged a lateral branch to become the apical shoot. Auxins play a key role in the behavior processes of plant life – it is the hormone that causes a plant to bend toward the sun – and in this case, it helped my balsam fir survive by propelling a new apical shoot upward.

Chemicals in the needles, which you may taste and chew, give balsams a unique defense against insects; they mimic a growth hormone that interferes with normal insect metamorphosis. Resins in the cone apparently have a deterrent effect against squirrels and seed feeding birds, such as the crossbill.

The largest balsam on record in the United States is in Fairfield, Pennsylvania. It stands one hundred feet tall and almost four feet in diameter. Even larger specimens exist in Canada, from Northern Canada south into the Great Lakes.

The other eastern fir is the *Abies frasei* or Fraser fir. The Fraser fir has a broader spread that balsam fir and is bedecked with bracts. It is quite similar to the balsam fir and also is used as Christmas trees. It was named by Scot botanist, John Fraser (1750-1811), who collected plants, saplings and seeds from North America, West Indies, and Russia under Catherine the Great. He explored the Eastern Seaboard on four separate visits.

Apparently, when hiking the highest of the Appalachian mountains, he encountered the celebrated French botanist, Andre Michaux (1746-1813), who in turn was discovering new plants for King Louis XVI. Together they identified and named countless flowers, shrubs, and trees, deriving the names from both Latin and French, e.g., azaleas, rhododendrons, and magnolias. The two men apparently did not get along. Michaux believed that Fraser was "dogging" his footsteps to be sure that the Crown got the naming rights for any new flower, shrub or tree. Offering the excuse that his horse had wandered off, Michaux allowed Fraser to trek ahead. That is how Fraser got the naming rights for the new tree he discovered alone, the Fraser (English) fir.

I have planted several of the firs species including Balsam fir, Fraser fir, Concolor fir, Korean fir, a golden-yellow Korean dwarf fir (*aurea*), and my Bristle cone fir. All planted in the thicket near M-25. Each species has its own peculiar scent, mixtures of lemon, turpentine or tangerine.

Abies concolor or white fir is the most forgiving fir, and a favorite of mine. Its striking feature is its colors, long blue-green foliage highlighted by blue-white new growth in spring, and turning whitish or powder blue by fall. The needles are up to two and a half inches long (long for a fir). It tolerates hot summers and cold winters. It too makes a great Christmas tree. The white fir will keep its needles for about ten years. Spruce on the other hand keep their needle for about six years, and pines keep their needles for about three years. The white fir will grow about a foot a year for up to ninety years. The United States national champion, found in Northern Utah, is ninety four feet tall. It purplish cones appear after—guess when? Forty years! Obviously, I have never seen them!

The Albert Holden Arboretum, Kirkland, Ohio, covering over 3,600 acres, includes Concolor firs among its almost 10,000 woody plant specimens. At its research center (yes, they have a research center), they indicated that, if the firs are planted in clay, they grow at two thirds the rate of those planted in loamy soil, yet they still grow. Concolors are striking cultivars.

A similar fir discovered by David Douglas is the *Abies procera* or noble fir, which has the biggest cones of any firs, and shorter and paler needles than the grand fir.

The other four species grow from Alaska south to California. They are the *Abies amabilis* or red silver fir; *Abies magnifica* or red fir; *Abies lasiocarpa* or alpine fir; *Abies bracteata* or bristlecone fir; and many dwarf variants.

The American botanist John Bartram (1699-1777) published the first book on American trees in 1785. Carl Linnaeus called Bartram the "greatest natural botanist in the world." Bartram corresponded with nearly all the great European botanists, as he explored the Alleghenies, the Catskills, the Carolinas, and Florida, in search of new trees, and was a friend of Benjamin Franklin. His book is a landmark in botany and contains several of the earliest descriptions of shrubs, trees, and firs.

In the 1800s, Dr. David Hosack (1769-1835), physician, botanist, and college professor, founded the first American botanical garden, the Elgin Botanic Garden, located where Rockefeller Center now stands. He tended to the fatal injuries of Alexander Hamilton after the duel with Aaron Burr. I find it more interesting that Dr. Hosack welcomed Sir David Douglas to the United States in 1823. The Douglas fir, my favorite tree, lines our driveway and "lines" the interior of our home!

David Douglas also discovered and introduced many *pinaceae*, such as the sugar pine, the noble fir, and the silver fir as well as my bonsai, the Sitka spruce (*Picea sitchensis*), which I bring into the house every winter.

ABIES GRANDIS
Grand Fir

It almost goes without saying that David Douglas discovered the biggest of all firs, *Abies grandis,* or grand fir. The grand fir aka giant fir, white fir, silver fir, Vancouver fir or Oregon fir, is the major constituent of the Ecoregion of the Cascade Range. John Muir waxed elegant over the firs of the Cascade Range. Upon gazing up to see the grand fir on Vancouver Island, I marveled at its beauty and size-reaching ninety meters or about 290 feet. It was love at first sight!

The leaves of the grand fir are straight, parallel-sided, and shiny mid-green. They are set on each side of the twig in flat rows, like the teeth of a comb. Their undersides have two pale blue lines, which you rarely see because the branches hang flat and low. Both staminate and pistillate cones occur on the same tree, but instead of dropping from the tree intact like most gymnosperms, the scales and attendant bracts drop, leaving the persistent spikelike axis. Very unique! Each scale bears a pair of small winged seeds, which the birds love.

Historically, the grand fir's bark has medicinal properties. It is also popular as a Christmas tree. Its lumber is a softwood, harvested as a "hem fir," used in paper making, construction, framing and flooring, wherever resistance to splitting and splintering is desired.

My grand fir, about ten years old, is in the thicket next to M-25. It is thriving.

ABIES KOREANA
Korean Fir

The profile of Abies includes beautiful firs from the Far East, particularly from China, Korea and Japan. My favorite is the Korean *Abies koreana* or Korean fir, of which I have two: one on the border of the southeast line and the other in the west thicket of trees near M-25. Hugh Johnson describes this eye-catching beauty as a "... decadent display of Faberge imitating confectionery in ivory and rubies, or scrambled eggs in amber and gold: they are plump, and piercing purple, with brown contour lines and spangles of translucent resin, and like presents in dreams they crumble when you pick them up." Korean fir is an evergreen conifer with a somewhat globe shaped habit of descending branches. It has glossy, deep green leaves with contrasting white lines on the underside, and bears attractive purple cones after ten years. It was introduced to the United States in 1918 by Ernest Wilson, a botanist at the Arnold Arboretum, Harvard. The tree there was over sixty-five feet tall and twenty-five feet wide when we last saw it. Now, assuming it is still growing, it must be ... tall.

My Korean dwarf fir boasts short bright yellow needles adorned with silvery undersides. I am delighted that, yes, my tree has produced cones since 2017. It is a slow grower, in part because it is partially shaded, but thriving.

Dwarf Korean yellow fir, Abies Koreana

Tsuga canadensis
Hemlock

Hemlocks are my all-time favorites with their massive trunks and wide branches. They are treasured by most gardeners and botanists and grow coast to coast. The United States champion is in the Great Smoky Mountains National Park and stands 165 feet tall and has a rugged trunk of almost six feet in diameter. I planted several hemlocks in 2004, transplanting a few saplings from Wayne Smith's property where he has a splendid grove of hemlocks, each about 150 feet tall, growing along the so-called Griggs creek north of Marilyn Manor. Behold the vertically grooved cinnamon-red, almost purplish chocolate colored bark. Delicious to the eye.

No, this tree is not related to the poisonous herb known as hemlock. On the contrary, Native Americans brewed a medicinal tea from the tree's leafy branchlets. Hemlocks were celebrated in the writing and poetry of Henry Wadsworth Longfellow (1807-1882). Favorites include "Paul Revere's Ride," "The Song of Hiawatha," "Evangeline" and below:

> This is the forest primeval. The murmuring pines and the hemlocks,
> Bearded with moss, and in garments green, indistinct in the twilight,
> Stand like Druids of eld, with voices sad and prophetic, Stand like harpers hoar, with beards that rest on their bosoms.

At intermediate altitudes such as the Appalachian mountains, hemlocks soar above the rest of the forest rising like church spires for as far as the eye can see. Besides loving shade, and the fact that it cannot be invaded or displaced by other species, it loves rocks, straddling them with ruddy roots, cracking them as it grows, rubbing its "knees" against great boulders. As Longfellow observed and heard, the hemlock tree whistles softly to itself, not roaring like a pine, but murmuring and sighing, not sorrowful but letting tranquility fall upon us. Without killing the tree, deer, rabbits and squirrels browse extensively on its foliage, leaving the seeds for the birds.

The most serious pest problem is the hemlock woolly adelgid, an aphid-like insect accidentally introduced from Asia. I controlled my infestation by introducing Japanese Lady Beetles, which are natural predators. These "ladybugs" eat the anchor threads holding the woolly adelgid's eggs onto the tree, dislodging them and causing them to fall harmlessly to the ground. I have not used any chemical controls on any of my trees.

Hemlocks are patient trees. They grow at moderate rates depending on local conditions, although I apply compost generously on my hemlocks to encourage faster growth. Talking about slow growth. Think of the hemlock that George Washington planted in 1791. According to Guy Sternberg, author of *Native Trees for North American Landscapes* (2004), an excellent reference, it has not yet reached thirty inches in diameter.

METASEQUOIA GLYPTOSTROIDES
Dawn Redwood

The dawn redwood once was a common tree in our landscape, fifty to one hundred million years ago when the dinosaurs roamed! Fossil records show that dawn redwoods were abundant across the Northern Hemisphere, including North America, Greenland, and Europe, but the tree was once thought to be extinct. The story of its rediscovery is as gripping as any melodrama.

In 1941, during World War II, the genus *Metasequoia*, meaning "like a sequoia," was described and reported by paleobotanist Shigeru Miki (1901-1974). He thought he had discovered the fossils of an extinct species because none of his fossils were less than 150 million years old.

In the same year, 1941, Kan Duo (Toh Kan) (1903-1961), professor of Forest Management, National Central University, China, observed living specimens while performing a survey in Sichuan and Hubei provinces. Unaware of Miki's new genus, he recorded the unique traits of the tree, but did not attempt to identify or publish his findings. Ignored but not forgotten! After the war in 1946, Professors Zheng Wanjun (Wan Chun Cheng) and Hu Xiansu (Hsen Hsu Hu), National Central University, made the pivotal connection between Miki's fossil gems and the living samples.

The plot thickens... In 1947, the Arnold Arboretum, Harvard University, provided $250 to fund an expedition by Zheng Wanjun's assistant Hua Jingchan (Ching-Shan Hwa) (b. 1921), to collect seeds from the trees in China. Hua Jingchan returned to Harvard on January 5, 1948 with several kilos, about four pounds. Arnold Arboretum distributed them to botanic gardens and universities all over the world. The dawn redwood is now a protected tree with legal status in China.

Guess what? We have two dawn redwoods thriving on our property.

Are all conifers evergreen? No! Remarkably, dawn redwoods are deciduous "conifers" that drop their needles every fall and regrow fresh green ones each spring. (Larch and bald cypress are also deciduous conifers.) The dawn redwood is a fast growing tree that typically reaches about one hundred feet tall with a twenty-five foot spread. Its bright green needles turn copper, almost rusty-apricot orange, in the fall, and the tree loses them until the following spring. The needles are arranged spirally and alternately on the twigs. While the bark and foliage are similar to other coastal redwoods, older trees (not mine yet), form wide buttresses on the lower trunk. The distinctive "armpit" under each branch is fissured, the bark there exfoliating cinnamon colored ribbon-like strips and strands. Although a magnificent giant of the tree world, its flowers are tiny, olive sized cones of dangling clusters along branch tips, a true survivor.

In 2000, upon the occasion of my retirement from First Lutheran Church of the Reformation, New Britain, Connecticut, my wife and children planted for me a dawn redwood in Walnut Hill Park New Britain. I like to think the seedling came from the Arnold Arboretum, Harvard. It's gorgeous and should live, God willing, for over three hundred years and reach a height of 120 to 200 feet.

Several people have asked me: "How tall will it grow?" and "Is it the tallest tree?" While dawn redwoods reach about 120 feet or more it is not a giant sequoia. The tallest tree in the world is the giant sequoia sempervirens, named "Hyperion," measuring 379.1 feet tall. It was discovered on August 25, 2006, in the Redwood National Park (designated a national park by President Carter). Stephen Sillett, Forest Canopy Scientist verified it as the tallest tree by scaling it and dropping a tape. It is estimated that the tree is over six hundred years old. It is still growing. The name Hyperion comes from one of the Titans of Greek mythology. Hyperion was the "high one," the god of heavenly light, and father of the lights of heaven: Eos the Dawn, Helios the Sun and Selene the Moon. The exact location of the Hyperion is kept secret to protect it from damage.

Recall the short story "The Jumping Frog of Calaveras County" by

Mark Twain, beloved storyteller? Well, in Calavaras County, California in 1852, a hunter named A.T. Dowd, became lost in the woods after following a wounded bear. He found himself in the midst of giant sequoia trees. News of the "discovery" spread and the trees become a tourist attraction, complete with a hotel. A giant sequoia, called "The Big Tree," was felled in 1853. It took five men twenty-five straight days to bring it down. Reportedly when it crashed down mud splashed about one hundred feet in the air. The trunk was measured at 302 feet long. Its rings were counted and the tree was verified as 1,300 years old. The stump measured thirty feet across and was actually used as a dance floor. No wonder the location of the Hyperion is a deep secret! Because the giant sequoia is protected, there is no commercial usage for its wood.

Talking about ancient trees, have you been into the swamps of the Okefenokee National Wildlife Refuge in Georgia? Not only can you expect birds, snakes, alligators, and carnivorous plants, but also beautiful bald cypress trees draped with ghostlike moss and alive with tree frogs. Botanists and scientists have identified bald cypress trees living on average two hundred to six hundred years with a height of 150 feet, with several recently discovered trees to be over one thousand years old.

We underestimate the value of trees because they are incredibly "slow." Their average life span, longer than our eighty to ninety years (knock on wood), can be about five times as long as ours. Several species, such as redwoods and quaking aspen, are thousands of years old. As Toni Morrison said: "Trees are like us, except they can't walk."

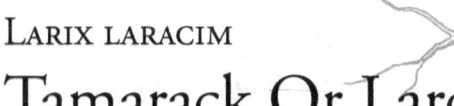

Larix laracim
Tamarack Or Larch

Our neighbor, Canada, is the world's second biggest country, at nearly ten million square kilometers, of which one third is a resplendent boreal forest. (The United States is third with over 9.8 million square kilometers.) Despite its size, the boreal forest boasts only nine species of trees, of which six are conifers: jack and lodgepole pines, black and white spruce, the balsam fir, and the larch known as tamarack. I have planted all of them. All of which are thriving! The other three are broadleaves: aspen, balsam poplar, and paper birch. Only these species can cope with northern winters. One of my favorites is the beautiful tamarack or larch tree.

The first time that I observed tamaracks was in the early 1960s in the Hiawatha National Forest, Schoolcraft County, Upper Peninsula. It was near our property in the cold of winter, and the trees looked dead lurking in a swamp. Seeing me blush apologetically, Leslie Bouschor, the Forest Superintendent at the time, assured me that the crisp corpselike forms, after the geese are gone from the beaver ponds and the snow is melted, would put forth unexpected blooms followed by full flowers. And indeed, it is a delicate charm, after my trees have dropped their needles, to observe the moment when the soft pale-green fresh needles clothe the military-like sternness of the bare branches with sparse tufts of foliage every spring.

I recall a fishing trip on Coat Tail Lake, in the Hiawatha National Forest, Schoolcraft County,

UP, near our property, with Sally and our newborn daughter, Jennifer. We caught several northern pikes, admired the firs, paper birch, northern white pines and enjoyed the scent of wild raspberries. Sally pan fried the pike and made rice for dinner at the home of Leslie Bouschor, where we stayed for several days. Mr. Bouschor was a French born Forest Superintendent who "homesteaded" the whole subdivision and was "grandfathered" into the National Forest. He became a friend who encouraged us to build a cottage next to his home.

We bought the property in September 1960, for $600 with $60 down and the balance due whenever! My recollection is when we paid only an additional $200, he gave us the deed for the property. The property # 77-004-450-027-50, has the following legal description: 991A SEC 29 T44N R17W LOT 27 OF BOUSCHOR'S SUB EXC THE S 200. It is about an acre on the National Historic Indian River, where I have planted a variety of saplings over the years.

Joseph Greaux, an Ojibwe whom Sally and I met planning three pow wows at the Sanilac County Historical Museum, shared with us that Native Americans used the roots of tamarack for sewing strips of birch bark into their beautiful canoes. He said that the "best roots" came from beaver ponds, for they were especially tough, pliant, slender and elongated. Mr. Greaux died in 2018.

John Josselyn (1638-1675), an English traveler to the Bay colonies under Governor John Winthrop, was a poet, writer and naturalist-historian who recorded: "The Turpentine that issuers forth from the larch or tamarack tree is singularly good to heal wounds, and to draw out the malices of any ache rubbing the place therewith."

For generations the Scots have loved larch or tamarack trees and I believe it is in their blood! The fourth Duke of Atholl was so smitten with tamaracks that he planted 17,000,000 them, including beside Dunkeld Cathedral on the banks of the Tay, about 1738-1740. At least doff your tam to thank him.

JUNIPERUS COMMUNIS
Common Juniper

Junipers have vastly varied growing habits and usually grow about five to ten feet tall at various points, with spreads just as wide. It grows prostrate, forming a ground cover. Juniper cones look like fleshy blueberries. They are edible and are sometimes used as a flavoring for gin. The word juniper comes from the French *genievre*, which is derived from the name of the tree, "genevrier." They are used as ornamental shrubs or as ground cover in rock garden or places where it is difficult to cultivate perennials.

The bark is thin, dark reddish brown and peels off into papery scales. The tree is dioecious, with only male or female cones on any individual plant. The common juniper is the only species which grows naturally in Europe, Asia, and America. Although quite common, let me quote Gertrude Jekyll (1843-1932), horticulturist and garden designer who created over four hundred gardens in the United Kingdom and the United States, who feels differently: "Its tenderly mysterious beauty of colouring, ...as delicately subtle in its own way of cloud or mist, or haze in warm, wet woodland. It has very little or positive green; a suspicion of warm colour in the shadowy hollows and a blue-grey bloom of the tenderest quality imaginable on the masses of foliage." She is so poetic, that I had to take a second and more detailed look at my own plants. She's right!

Incidentally, all common juniper could be called retinospora, having nothing but juvenile foliage. Other juniper species are more variable, having some adult branches along with the individual sprays of fine sharp-pointed leaves, which are the juvenile branches.

We have a common juniper and a *J.virginiana* or eastern red cedar.

There are hundreds of cultivars of common and eastern red cedar junipers. Nurseries tend to concentrate on the narrower, smaller trees, looking for shapeliness, although there are hundreds of other popular varieties. As recently as 1930, another drooping juniper species was discovered in the Burmese foothills of the Himalayas, *J. recurva* "Cox" named after Euan Cox, its finder. It looks like a weeping willow at a distance, with its long camouflage-green sprays hanging from arching branches. Almost mystical looking. The sprays are so dense and soft to the touch that you can squeeze them like sponges.

Eastern red cedar and common juniper are among our most valuable wildlife trees and shrubs. Cedar waxwings earned their name for their preference for the tree's fruit or berries. We have observed them on an Audubon tour, feasting and "staggering around" the trees for over an hour, as if enjoying flavored "gin and tonic." Over forty other wildlife species depend heavily upon the juniper for food. The dense foliage furnishes protective cover for nesting sites. We also saw the iridescent olive hairstreak butterfly "chasing birds" on the Audubon tour.

Care to join us for a tour? Bring your highball glass with ice cubes, a wedge of lime or lemon, tonic water of your choice and we will add a few jiggers of Beefeater or Botanist gin.

Eastern Red Cedar

Everyday things, including trees, get the least amount of attention! Red cedar wood is everywhere if you look for it—fences, shingles, furniture, coffins, and boats. Early settlers in the thumb were often referred to as shingle shavers (and raspberry pickers). Maybe that is why, without question or discussion, we built the exterior of our home with red cedar planks, thrice stained, by Sally and me, and thrice painted by Larry Hooper and his son, Chad, over the last twenty years.

With its endurance and strength, a red cedar will grow for three hundred years given even, moderate climactic conditions and just about any soil. Farmers often planted red cedars as a windbreak along one side of the farmyard and lined the driveways to their homes with them. The earliest explorers to reach Roanoke Island in 1564, specifically Arthur Barlowe and Philip Amides, described red cedars as "the tallest and reddest Cedars in the world." When log cabins arrived on the scene, red cedar was a favorite. In old graveyards and even new cemeteries, red cedar assists the imagination as they appear to be pointing to heaven; their evergreen boughs speak symbolically of life eternal.

Can you remember Faber pencils? For over a century, 70-90 percent of every red cedar log was wasted just to make lightweight pencils which could be sharpened with ease. Eventually, the slogan for the orchardists, "cedar or cider," was changed to "cider or pencils," according to Donald Peattie, (1898-1964) in *A Natural History of Trees*. Red cedar wood also produces medicinal aerosols that protect clothes from wool-eating moths and is often used to line closets, and indeed we have a cedar closet in our own home. It is also used commercially for its oils and perfumes.

So common are red cedars that today most people—including me—don't notice the blue berries or fleshy cones on the female trees, even though there can be over one million of them on a healthy tree. The colors of the berries and cones progress from a pale, frosted bluegreen, to steel blue, to bluish black.

Not only are these blue berries gorgeous on the trees, but, more importantly they are a food source for birds. Think of any of the fruit-eating birds, blue jays, crows, robins, bluebirds, goldfinches, flickers, grosbeaks... all of which regularly feed on our trees and feeders. Are they edible, you ask? Although they have been used medicinally and as flavoring for centuries, they are listed as poisonous by poison control centers, so eating in large quantities is not recommended.

The male trees produce yellow pollen in brown and scaly shingled cones. Botanists refer to these male or pollen cones as *strobili* which are about the size of rice grains but look like shingled or plaited foliage appearing on the tip of nearly every branchlet. In March winds I have seen red cedars "go up in yellowish smoke," which can be startling!

Never have I seen the "flowers" that precede the cones, not even after looking at them, as I am not sure what I am looking for or at. In a delightful book by Nancy Hugo, entitled *Seeing Trees*, she quotes Walter E. Roger's *Tree Flowers of Forest, Park and Street*: "Among Gymnosperms, the red cedar, next to the Ginkgo, offers perhaps the flower hardest to recognize as such. The lack of a strongly differentiating color, the minuteness of the parts, the apparent similarity to the foliage—all conspire to conceal from an observer the true nature of the flower." Incentive enough for me to look—but to no avail. The real "kicker" is that my real motive in looking for the flowers was to see the olive hairstreak butterfly which feeds on red cedar foliage almost exclusively. Its wings are beautiful with a green patina and bronzy brown and white markings—supposedly. Neither Nancy Hugo nor I have ever seen it...

Red cedars are often disfigured by galls of a fungal disease which in turn infect the leaves of apple trees. Neither the disease nor the chronic rust it causes is fatal to either tree, although a nontoxic treatment is required for apple orchards. But, and how is this for overkill, the 1918 Annual Report of the Virginia State Horticultural Society writes:

"Cedar eradication is the cheapest form of orchard insurance that you can buy. The cost of the average is less than the cost of a single spare application." Yet, I have never seen any galls or fungus on any of our several red cedars—and we even have several species of apple trees.

Many shrublike cultivars serve as ground cover, and in terms of garden design, the red cedar and other junipers are the most flexible, literally.

I learned this firsthand. In 2002, one of my trees, a fifteen foot red cedar, was "toppled" by a severe ice storm. It was flattened out (90 degrees) and frozen to the ground with ice and icicles for over a week. And then the ice thawed and it began to straighten up...slowly. Its cellulose, a polysaccharide of glucose which constitutes fibrous parts of the cell walls of plants, and lignin, an amorphous polymer that provides rigidity to plants and trees, cooperated perfectly – as they thawed those two constituent parts restored the tree to its glory!

You may recall that we visited British Columbia in 2018 to visit our granddaughter, Andy, and Sally's Aunt, her Dad's sister, Auntie Lucia, her son and daughter-in-law, Ray and Myline and their son, Gerard. We marveled at the size of the western red cedar or Pacific red cedar, which grow up to 200 to 230 feet tall and 9.8 to13.1 feet in trunk diameter! It's overwhelming in its size, the beauty of its pleated leaves, and its ability to live well over a thousand years. Truly an *Arbor Vitae* or "tree of life" for the aboriginal or indigenous nations. There are almost two hundred clans/tribes in British Columbia. These indigenous nations cut the largest specimen for totems, canoes, dwellings, and furniture as well lath, shingles, sleds, and even clothing if you include soft absorbent bark diapers.

Unfortunately, the western red cedar does not grow in the Michigan clime. Therefore, I have saved samples of western cedar to remind us of its value.

The summer of our visit, Andy was a junior at UBC. Andy led us to museums, parks and, oh yes, restaurants. She joined us on a guided tour of the university campus and museum which introduced us to a fabulous collection of Native American art, paintings, wooden sculptures and artifacts. That experience piqued our interest in visiting a Native American village of the Squamish band, about two thousand strong, in British Columbia. Small family-based bands moved from Asia to America about 30,000-12,000 years ago by land, because sea levels were low enough to create a land bridge, or by sailing from Polynesia.

For a day, we visited with the Squamish Nation, exploring a Native American museum and a logging camp on the Ocean. When visiting the Squamish Village, we joined a tour with a German architect under contract with the Squamish Nation to design a "shopping center," motel and a larger modern museum—all out of wood, primarily western Cedar. As we chatted, he shared that his specialty was wooden structures in Germany and that's why he was very pleased to have been awarded the contract.

After our new house was built, Sally and I congratulated each other for a herculean job well done and bought a carving made of western red cedar to commemorate the occasion. A hand carved "family" of five salmons by a Haida artist adorns our stone fireplace. Are they Chinook (King), Chum (Dog), Coho (Silver), or Sockeye (Pink) Salmon? Ask our son, Mark, who worked in a salmon cannery in Dillingham, Alaska, one summer while a student at the University of Alaska, Fairbanks.

When I retired in 2001, our three children purchased me a handcrafted, made in Canada, sixteen-foot cedar rowboat. A real work of art which begged the question, ought we keep it in our living room?

When Mark and Patty graduated from the University of Alaska, Fairbanks in 1987, I planted an Alaska cedar in commemoration of their degrees. Often mistaken for a cedar, as evidenced by the name Alaska cedar, Alaska yellow cedar or Nootka cedar, *Cupressus nootkatensis* aka Alaska cypress is actually a species of trees in the cypress family native to the coastal northwestern North America, specifically Washington, Alaska, and British Columbia. Now arguments favor a new classification, *Callitropsis nootkatensis*, confirmed by botanists as a subgenus. Stay tuned as it may change again! Nonetheless, by any name, the magnificent tree is doing well on the northern property line on the lake side of our house.

It will grow up to 130 feet tall with evergreen pendulous branches bearing one quarter inch dark green scale-like leaves. A guide in British Columbia pointed us to a "beauty," about 1,800 years old! Like other cypress and cedar, it is durable, resistant to weather and insects, and does well in various types of soil. The wood itself turns and carves quite well, and can be used for exterior siding, shingles, decking, laminated beams, paneling cabinetry and is especially good for millwork needed for historic restoration.

Callitropsis nootkatensis, aka Alaska cypress, Nootka cedar, yellow cedar, Alaska cedar or Alaska yellow cedar

Thuja occidentalis
American Arborvitae

Native to the forests of both North America and Asia, American arborvitae is a member of the cypress family, and is primarily a Canadian tree. It is known for its slender habit and dense glossy foliage. The Arborvitae is a compact tree that seldom attains the status of its related conifers, yet can surprise us by its beauty with easy care under optimal conditions. The United States national champion in Leelanau County, Michigan, is 113 feet tall and 5.7 feet in diameter. There are other arborvitae of comparable and larger sizes in Canada. Under "normal" conditions it can live about four hundred years.

American arborvitae seed cones, both male and female strobili, are borne on separate twigs of the same tree. The female strobili grow into oval, pea-sized seed cones with a few overlapping scales, ripening to a warm brown in late summer. Quite unique. Its thin bark is light brown, and cracks into ridges with frayed-out stringy edges. The branches are smooth, red and shiny.

The first record of an American tree being grown in Europe is from 1553, almost two hundred years before North American trees make a great impression on the world's botanists and gardens. Jacque Cartier brought a *Thuja occidentalis* to Paris. He first encountered the tree during his voyage through the St. Lawrence seaway in 1535-36.

During the voyage, the whole ship's crew had fallen deathly sick of scurvy, the plague of that day's sailing vessels. But then, Cartier encountered Domagaia, aka Chief Donnacona, from (now) Quebec City, a Native American. Just ten days before, Cartier had seen

Domagaia deathly ill with scurvy, writing that his "legs were swollen and his teeth spoiled, his gums rotten and stinking."

> Now, the "Captaine seeing him and whole and sound, was thereat marvelous glad, hoping to understand and know of him how he had healed himself, to the end that might ease and help his men." Domagaia replied: "They had taken the juice and sappy of the leaves of a certain tree." Then our Captaine asked of him if any were to be had thereabout, desiring him shew him. ...Domagaia straight sent two women to fetch some of it, which brought ten or twelve branches of it, and therewithal shewed the way how to use it, and that it is thus, to take the barke and leaves of the sayd tree, and boil them together, then drink of the sayd decoction every day, and to put the dregs of it upon his legs that is sick."

Even though Cartier could not understand it then, his men were cured of scurvy by vitamin C from the arborvitae sap. Thus thereafter was the tree known as arborvitae: *arbor* meaning tree, *vitae* meaning life...the tree of life.

Even before the 16th century, Native Americans left offerings at a natural shrine known as the "Witch Tree." This ancient tree grows on the exposed rock of Hat Point along the northward coast of Lake Superior, across from Isle Royale. The old, crooked arborvitae served as a landmark for centuries and was noted by explorer Sieur de la Verendrye as he passed by it in 1731.

Native Americans, especially those in Alaska, often used the soft wood of arborvitae in making the rough-hewn rafters and joists of "primitive dwellings." They also used the tree to make blankets, ropes, fishing equipment, and harness rigging for dog sled teams. Truly it is a "tree of life."

Within its natural habitat, arborvitae tolerates urban pollution conditions and heat as long as its roots are in cool, moist soil. Scale insects and spider mites can take their toll on these trees, but normally the trees recover. They ought to be bagged over winter in colder climes to protect the tree from drying wind and cold temperatures.

Our previous neighbors to the north, William and Mary Schmidt, planted numerous arborvitae trees to serve as a screen on the property line. These plants are still doing well. I planted a dwarf gold arborvitae with a round habit in our courtyard. Another *occidentalis* is growing under the Japanese maple tree in the midst of our circular driveway against the flanks of a classic golden conifer, "Rheingold," which at about twelve feet, is reaching its maximum.

Arborvitae are extensively used in cities, homes and courtyards for landscaping. There are many similar and related species, such as the western red cedar, Atlantic white cedar, and the Arizona cypress, each of which will grace any home or estate for years.

TAXUS BACCATA

Yew

Yew trees have the distinction of being the darkest green of all the conifers. In autumn, if both male and female plants are grown, they will produce small, poisonous berries. They keep their needles through the winter. The name "yew" comes from the German word *ewig*, meaning "everlasting." The fruit-like arils or berries are mainly red but can be of various colors. These seeds are dispersed by birds. Over one hundred cultivars exist, including Japanese yew, *Taxus cuspidata,* which means "multi-stemmed." Yews range in size from tiny shrubs to sixty feet trees. All yews have narrow, very dark green needles which grow very slowly. Our yew, at the northwest corner of the garage, is probably an English yew.

Yews are regularly shown in English gardens as a perfect background for colorful shrubs and perennials. There is often fierce competition over the scale and sagginess of the hedges that adorn stately homes and estates. Yews have been planted in Britain, including Wales, Scotland and Ireland, for over three hundred years.

According to Colin Tudge, botanist, scientist, and author of a great resource book, *The Secret Life of Trees* (2005), there is a yew still growing in Scotland under which Pontius Pilate may have slept. Yews of course are long lived, but perhaps this outlandish claim is speculative. Most sources say the yew can live up to six hundred years, at most. So I looked into the Scottish "myth." I discovered that the "Fortingall Yew" is thought to be between 3,000 and 9,000 years old!

During the Hundred Years War between England and France

(1337-1453), the English utilized traditional longbows constructed from yew wood. The English preferred yews over all other types of wood for longbows. Its strength, lightness and flexibility allowed the English soldier to bend his bow. The Frenchman drew the bow of the crossbow differently, and it was often too heavy to lift. An English bishop, Hugh Latimer (1490-1555), a reformer and scholar said of a French soldier with crossbow: "Keeping his right hand at rest upon the nerve, he rested his whole weight of his body into the horns of his bow."

In the major Battle of Agincourt, the weapon proved decisive as the English, 5,000 strong and backed up by a mere nine hundred longbow-equipped archers, defeated 20,000 French mounted knights dressed in masterpieces of armor. The longbow possessed both long range and accuracy, and specialized arrowheads were developed so that the arrows could even pierce chainmail and light armor, killing horses as well. Unimaginable! No wonder the huge increase in the English army's need for yews. By 1473, Edward IV decreed compulsory yew imports, but the fast-rising demand for the wood proved unsustainable. On October 26,1595, Elizabeth I decreed that henceforth the army should replace longbows with guns, even though the bow was still the much more effective weapon. The remaining wild yews could continue their slow journey into immortality.

Yews are widely associated with church yards and cemeteries. I am not sure why, although I have heard various explanations over the years. "They're green all winter." "The berries are poisonous." "They live forever." "They're so solemn." And even simply, "My grandfather planted them."

A favorite poem of mine is found in an old book by the botanist Julia Rogers (1866-1958), *The Tree Book* (1905). In volume nine of the almost six hundred page long substantive series, she shares a description of how branches of yew were gathered to deck English cottages when a body lay awaiting burial. The mourners' heads were bound with yew branches and they draped more branches over the casket. She recounted the poem "The New Sirens—A Palinode" by Matthew Arnold (1822 – 1888), oft recited at funerals:

Pluck, pluck cypress, O pale maidens,
Dusk, O dusk the hall with yew! Weep, and wring
Every hand; and every head Bind with cypress and
sad yew
For him that was of men most true.

Could anything be sadder?

Ginkgo Biloba
or Maidenhair Tree

Ginkgo, also spelled gingko, is the only species in its family. It is one of the oldest living species, having survived the continental drift, about 260-270 million years ago. It may have also survived the dinosaurs because it appears nearly identical to fossils from the ice age! The tree originated in China, and it has been told that Buddhist monks saved it from extinction because they grew them in monastery gardens. Its name means "silver apricot" in Chinese and refers to its white nuts. The monks would serve the nuts on specials occasions as a vegetarian dish. Today, it is a Chinese delicacy, and the nuts can be roasted as a confection or appetizer. Chinese writings from the twelfth century mention the tree in its natural state, and literature from the 16th century refers to the tree as the duck's foot tree, referring to the shape of the leaves. The maidenhair tree may attain a height anywhere from fifty to eighty feet and can live 1,000 years. Astounding. I love the tree's fan-shaped leathery leaves when they turn bright yellow, really almost golden, in autumn.

The tree is dioecious. The female tree's seeds are light yellow-brown and have large fleshly outer layers which contain butyric acids, aka butanoic acid. They smell like rancid butter or vomit, not too pleasant.

Many folks have found out the hard way that they are allergic or sensitive to the chemical in this coating, *sarcotesta*. Touching it results in contact dermatitis or blisters similar to poison ivy. Ginkgo leaf extract is marketed as a dietary supplement for high blood pressure, cognitive decline, macular degeneration and altitude sickness, but without any medical evidence. My three trees are all male so if you are looking for seeds, you're out of luck.

Engelbert Kaempfer (1651-1716), German physician, explorer, botanist, and author, was the first in Europe to write about the ginkgo. Kaempfer wrote *Flora Japanica* after touring Asia with the Dutch East Indies Company. The book was published in 1727, posthumously. Kaempfer's writings were the chief source of information about Japan after Japan closed its borders to the West during the 18th and 19th centuries. The first ginkgo arrived in Utrecht, the Netherlands in 1730. By 1754, several were growing in Kew Gardens, London, where they still grow. William Hamilton (1735-1840) brought the ginkgo to the United States, planted it on what is now the three hundred-acre Woodlands National Historic Landmark, complete with a Georgian mansion and arboretum, near Philadelphia.

Ginkgo is widely planted on city streets as an ornamental tree. It thrives in most soil conditions, and is not damaged by fungi or insects because no insects evolved with it. The design of the leaf has not changed and appears the same as fossilized leaves found in North Dakota. These fossils are part of the evidence that the ginkgo grew worldwide before the tree eventually retreated to the mountains of China. I have great respect for this marvelous tree, evolving as it has and surviving against all odds. Gingkos even survived the atomic bombing of Hiroshima. Six tenacious trees, now protected, are still growing 0.62 miles to 1.25 miles from ground zero, where no other plants or animals survived. The charred yet surviving ginkgo trees have become a shrine. We can ponder and meditate on the historic events "witnessed" by the ginkgo.

On my eightieth birthday, we planted two ginkgos at St. Paul Lutheran Church, Port Huron, on both driveways.

Ginkgo biloba

Epilogue

As a house guest once remarked: "What good is one tree?" My answer: "It's home to a Downy Woodpecker. If you take care of the birds, they will take care of the rest!"

Tending to our trees through the seasons and through the years, I have learned a lot. Living on Lake Huron, I have a special awareness of water. I see and know that trees lift and transpire vast amounts of water. Mature trees lift hundreds of liters of water every day! They are truly green oceans, transpiring water upward, defying gravity, helping moisture condense into rain. Yet my patch of wilderness begs more questions than we have yet learned how to ask.

Rising temperatures, changes in seasonality, altered rainfall and lake levels, all these things have enormous consequences for trees and wildlife. They lead to permanent shifts in plant and animal species, disrupting their finely tuned interdependence.

Most scientists and botanists fear that trees—name your favorite tree—are falling victim to the environmental degradations of global warming and acid rain. The drying effects, including the most obvious, fires, produce abnormal concentrations of greenhouse gases which may eliminate beeches (my favorite tree at the moment). Our biota, all flora and fauna, continue to be stressed by environmental degradation.

How do we minimize these trends? I believe trees are key-players in mitigating the effects of climate crises. Our trees need advocates before it is too late!

John Muir (1838-1914), Scottish-American, naturalist, author, philosopher, advocate, co-founder of the Sierra Club and known as the

"Father of National Parks," having helped establish Yosemite National Park and others, said: "During a man's life, only saplings can be grown, … replace the old trees—tens of centuries old—which haven't been destroyed…God has cared for these trees, saved them from drought, disease, leveling tempests and floods; but He cannot save them from fools."

Think about it, when was the last time you cleaned insects off your auto windshield after a trip? With climate change and loss of habitat, there is an apocalypse of birds and insects, which exhorts us to follow Greta Thurnberg's (b. 2003) warning about the climate crisis. Protect and feed the birds and plant a tree!

How we confront the climate crises depends on us. As Bruce Stein, the Chief Scientist, National Wildlife Federation, admonishes: "Avoid the unmanageable and manage the unavoidable."

Or as Pogo declared: "We are confronted with insurmountable opportunities."

Bill and Sally[7]

The author showing results of good sun, soil, and water

---

[7] © Lifetouch Photography/ Barber Photography, Sandusky Michigan. Express permission (limited copyright release) granted to author.

Selected References by Author

American Horticultural Society. *Plants That Merit Attention*. Vol. 2, *Scrubs*. Timber Press, 2000.

Armitage, Allan. *Native Plants*. Timber Press, 2006.

Beresford-Kroeger, Diana. *Arboretum Borealis*. The University of Michigan Press, 2010.

Calthrop, Dior Clayton. *A Diary of an Eighteenth-Century Garden*. London: Williams and Norgate, no publication date stated.

Capon, Brian. *Botany for Gardeners*. Timber Press, 2015.

Chalker-Scott, Linda. *How Plants Work*. Timber Press, 2015.

Chamovitz, Daniel. *What a Plant Knows*. Scientific American/Farr, Straus and Giroux, 2012.

Coombes, Allen. *Trees*. Dorling Kindersley, 1992.

Dirr, Michael. Dirr's *Hardy Trees and Shrubs*. Timber Press, 2000.

Eastman, John. *Forest and Thicket*. Stackpole Books, 1992.

Fortey, Richard. *The Wood for the Trees*. Vintage Books of Penguin Random House, 2016.

Gossler, Roger, Eric Gossler and Marjory Gossler. *Gossler Guide to the Best Hardy Shrubs*. Timber Press, 2009.

Grimm, William Carey. *The Illustrated Book of Trees*. Stackpole Books, 2002.

Hessayon, D.G. *The Evergreen Expert*. London: Transworld Publishers, 1998.

Hobbs, Kevin and David West. *The Story of Trees*. London: Laurence King Publishers, 2020.

Hugo, Nancy Ross. *Seeing Trees*. Timber Press, 2011.

Huikari, Olavi. *The Miracle of Trees*. Bloomsbury Press, 2012.

Johnson, Hugh. *The World of Trees*. University of California Press, 2010.

Kroetsch, Robert. *Seed Catalogue*. Winnipeg, Canada: Turnstone Press, 1977 and 2004.

Kilmer, Joyce. *Trees and Other Poems*. Doubleday Doran and Company, 1914.

Lacy, Allen. *The Inviting Garden*. Henry Holt Company, 1998.

Leopold, Aldo. *A Sand County Almanac*. Ballantine Books, Round River, 1953.

Logan, William Bryant. Oak: The Frame of Civilization. W.W. Norton and Company, 2005.

Ogden, Scott and Lauren Springer Ogden. *Plant-driven Design*. Timber Press, 2008.

Paterson, Allen. *Best Trees For Your Garden*. Firefly Book, 2003.

Peattie, Donald Culross. *A Natural History of Trees*. Houghton Mifflin Company, 1991.

Pollen, Michael, *Second Nature*. Grove Press, 1998.

Qing, Li. *Forest Bathing (Shinrin Yoku)*. Timber Press, 2018.

Hillier Gardener's Guide to Trees and Shrubs. Reader's Digest Association, 1995.

Rehder, Alfred. *Manual of Cultivated Trees and Shrubs*. Dioscorides Press, 1987.

Rogers, Elizabeth Barlow. *Writing the Garden*. David R. Godine Publisher, 2011.

Rogers, Julia Ellen. *The Tree Book*. Vol. 9. Doubleday, Page and Company, 1916.

Robbins, Jim. *The Man Who Planted Trees*. Spiegl and Grau, 2002.

Rutkow, Eric. *American Canopy*. Scribner, 2012.

Sternberg, Guy and Jim Wilson. *Native Trees for North American Landscapes*. Timber press, 2004.

Suzuki, David and Wayne Grady. *Tree*. Greystone Books, 2004.

Symonds, George. *The Tree Identification Book*. Harper Collins, 1958.

Tripp, Kim and J.C. Raulston. *The Year in Trees*. Timber Press, 1997.

Tudge, Colin. *The Tree*. Three Rivers Press, 2005.

———, *The Secret Life of Trees*. Penguin Books, 2005.

Wohlleben, Peter. *The Hidden Life of Trees*. Greystone Books, 2015.

About the Author

William G. Moldwin is a bi-vocational community organizer, social worker, Lutheran pastor, and an advanced master gardener who holds an MBA. His career history includes work effecting social change via fundraising millions of dollars for community projects. Throughout his lifetime, he has reveled in planting trees. Now retired, Moldwin resides in Sanilac County, Michigan. This is his first book.